FEMINIST WEED FARMER

FEMINIST WEED FARMER

GROWING MINDFUL MEDICINE IN YOUR OWN BACK YARD

MADRONE STEWART

Microcosm Publishing
Portland, OR

FEMINIST WEED FARMER
Growing Mindful Medicine in Your Own Back Yard

Part of the DIY Series

© Madrone Stewart, 2018, 2020
This edition © Microcosm Publishing, 2018, 2020
First Edition, 3,000 copies, First published Sept 11, 2018
Second printing, 3000 copies, June 2020
Third printing, 3000 copies, June 2022

ISBN 978-1-62106-021-5
This is Microcosm #212
Cover by Cecilia Granata
Book design by Joe Biel

For a catalog, write or visit:
Microcosm Publishing
2752 N Williams Ave.
Portland, OR 97227
(503)799-2698
www.Microcosm.Pub

To join the ranks of high-class stores that feature Microcosm titles, talk to your local rep:
In the U.S. **Como** (Atlantic), **Fujii** (Midwest), **Book Travelers West** (Pacific), **Turnaround**
in Europe, **UTP/Manda** in Canada, **New South** in Australia, and **GPS** in Asia, Africa, India,
South America, and other countries. We are sold in the gift market by **Gifts of Nature.**

If you bought this on Amazon, I'm so sorry because you could have gotten it
cheaper and supported a small, independent publisher at www.Microcosm.Pub

Global labor conditions are bad, and our roots in industrial Cleveland in the 70s and
80s made us appreciate the need to treat workers right. Therefore, our books are
MADE IN THE USA.

Library of Congress Cataloging-in-Publication Data

Names: Stewart, Madrone, author.
Title: Feminist weed farmer : growing mindful medicine in your own backyard /
  Madrone Stewart.
Description: Portland, OR : Microcosm Publishing, 2018.
Identifiers: LCCN 2018010750 | ISBN 9781621060215 (pbk.)
Subjects: LCSH: Cannabis. | Marijuana--Therapeutic use.
Classification: LCC SB295.C35 S74 2018 | DDC 633.7/9--dc23
LC record available at https://lccn.loc.gov/2018010750

MICROCOSM · PUBLISHING

Microcosm Publishing is Portland's most diversified publishing house and distributor with a focus on the colorful, authentic, and empowering. Our books and zines have put your power in your hands since 1996, equipping readers to make positive changes in your life and in the world around you. Microcosm emphasizes skill-building, showing hidden histories, and fostering creativity through challenging conventional publishing wisdom. What was once a distro and record label was started by Joe Biel in his bedroom and has become among the oldest independent publishing houses in Portland, OR. In a world that has inched to the right for 80 years, we are carving out a place in the center with DIY skills, food, bicycling, gender, self-care, and social justice.

TABLE OF CONTENTS

Introduction

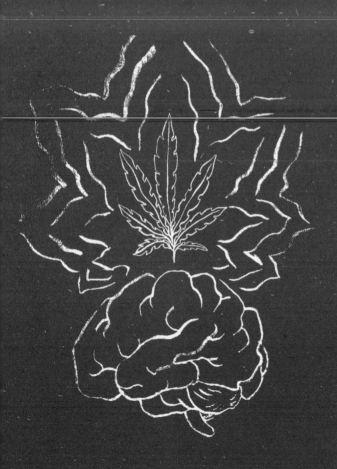

Cannabis is a powerful plant medicine that can be used to cultivate personal, cultural, and social transformation. Being stoned shifts our perspective; it expands our consciousness and helps us to see, with more clarity, who we are and the cultures in which our lives are embedded. It can also inspire creativity and the process of visioning, which are at the heart of any deep transformation. For women, this experience of expanded consciousness, insight, and stimulated creativity can be profoundly feminist. This altered state of consciousness can also help us to see oppressive cultural practices more clearly, as well as the process of challenging those practices. Perhaps most importantly, cannabis can help us develop a vision for ourselves and our societies beyond these unjust practices.

I believe that in order to consume cannabis with integrity, we must derive our plant medicine from ethically responsible sources. The current cannabis market, which is a blend of black market dealers and corporate controlled dispensaries, is completely market-driven and is not in line with feminist, environmentalist, or social justice values. Unfortunately, there is no reliable way for you to know where and how your medicine was produced, whether you buy it from a dispensary or a friend. Your medicine could have been grown in a warehouse and coated in pesticides sprayed by someone who is paid $10/hr, or it might have been organic, grown under the sun by a commune of radical, queer folks of color. However, because of the nature of the industry, there is no way for you to know anything about how your cannabis was produced. Therefore, I want to encourage all consumers—especially women, queer folks, and people of color who are so excluded from the cannabis industry—to consider growing your own plant medicine in line with your principles.

At its greatest, I believe that a feminist experience is when a woman becomes entirely the person that she needs to be. Cannabis, DMT, mushrooms, ayahuasca, and LSD, among other entheogenic plants and compounds, can help us to illuminate these invisible prisons that society has created for us, which prevent us from thriving. I believe that growing and getting high on cannabis and other psychedelics can help wake us up to who we are, how society is actively constraining our dreams, and they can help us illuminate pathways to liberation and self-actualization.

The source of great cognitive dissonance for many cannabis consumers is that this transformative medicine is often produced and sold by sources that are highly mysterious at best and explicitly unethical at worst. The majority of the contemporary U.S. cannabis industry does not embody the principles and values of feminism, environmentalism, and/or social justice. The industry is completely market-driven and overwhelmingly dominated by capitalist, straight, white, cis men. I love my straight white brothers, but I do not think it is fair that they have come to control this industry, especially since a disproportionate number of Black and brown people have been incarcerated for cultivating and selling pot throughout the span of the war on drugs. This is also especially infuriating because mothers have been penalized by both the criminal justice system and child protective services for cultivating and selling weed. In essence, they have received greater penalty for the same crimes. What a shameful reality, where the same people who have been disproportionately policed and penalized for cultivating cannabis have been left out of the industry now that it is legal and extremely lucrative. Some activists are organizing to make the industry more inclusive, which is an exciting development. However, in addition to the lack of diversity, legally sanctioned corporate cannabis factories are increasingly replacing "mom and pop" farms and pot shops, and thus the centralization of wealth and power within the industry is rapidly increasing.

Because of the increasingly grim and ethically abhorrent nature of the cannabis industry, I believe that all people should consider growing their own plant medicine. We desperately need to decentralize and diversify who is growing one of the most important medicines available to humanity. We cannot end up with a small handful of corporations growing our weed indoors, using extremely energy-intensive cultivation methods, and coating them with toxic chemicals. I especially believe that women, queer folks, and folks of color should grow our own psychedelic medicine because of how radically excluded we are from the emerging cannabis industry. I deeply believe that we need to empower ourselves with the skills and knowledge to grow the plants that help us to develop the wisdom that we need to liberate ourselves and our communities. We must stop supporting industries that are excluding our participation and are working against our values. This includes the emerging cannabis industry.

I believe that you, dear reader, can grow the dankest[1], stickiest, tastiest, loudest[2], highest-vibration cannabis on the planet. I believe that, together with the support of your friends and family, you can free yourself from the stranglehold of dispensaries by growing your own beautiful pot plants. I want to breathe life into your dream. I believe that you were born to take the power in your heart, mind, skin, and bones and use it to make great art, build beautiful relationships, and grow amazing plants. I want weed, kale, tomatoes, sunflowers, and echinacea cultivated in every backyard, terrace, and rooftop. I would love for the corporate controlled cannabis farms to fail, and I would love to see women and gender-queer cultivators put them out of business. This will only happen if we all roll up our sleeves and sow our own seeds of insight, freedom, beauty, and dignity. I believe that psychological freedom goes hand in hand with economic freedom from corporations. This includes corporate controlled dispensaries, which are proliferating throughout states where cannabis is now legally grown and sold. The only way to economically

---

1 Dank in this context means really high quality.
2 People use the word "loud" to describe the degree of smell. If your flowers are loud, they have a strong smell. If they are quiet, they do not have much of a smell. Most people prefer weed with a really strong smell. This might be because the terpenes create an "entourage effect," which makes the THC more therapeutically viable, i.e. the weed can actually get you higher. The entourage effect is the synergistic relationship between THC, CBD, and plant terpenes, including myrcene, limonene, and pinene.

free yourself from corporate cannabis is by growing your own or helping a friend.

In the guide that follows, I provide very simple instructions for growing organic, sun-grown cannabis. In addition, I generously dole out my biased beliefs from cover to cover. In addition to believing that consuming psychoactive plants can be a mentally liberating and empowering feminist experience and practice, I also believe that you should grow your cannabis with love and respect for the earth. This means growing without lights, without synthetic fertilizers or synthetic pesticides. I believe that you should pay close attention to your water usage and your use of supplies, especially those made out of plastic. I believe that as you learn how to grow, you should empower others—especially other women, queer folks, and folks of color—to grow their own as well.

If you follow these pages closely, you will have more than enough information to grow your own weed. However, I will warn you that once you start growing, it is tough to stop. Not only is it fun—at the end of the year you end up with lots of delicious weed that you can share with friends! There are also new ideas and experiments that you will want to try year after year.

This is a book written for beginners. It will provide you with a very simple method of growing that will get you through season one and perhaps season two. Once you have a few seasons under your belt, you will want to start adding your own spice to your grow, whether that means learning how to make your own compost, how to grow your own plant-based fertilizers, or how to light dep your plants. Trust me, I want for you to learn all about permaculture and Korean natural farming, but not in your first year. Keep it simple and develop your own method of cultivating over your lifetime. Also, if you aren't dripping with wealth, I suggest starting with no more than six plants and expanding over time if you so desire. Growing can be expensive, and the more plants you grow, the greater the cost.

I strongly recommend that you take some time and set clear intentions for your grow before you order seeds or start forking soil. These intentions can help to guide you throughout the season and can help you assess whether or not this project is what you intended it to be. This year my intentions were for the thriving of my garden, my relationships with my gardening crew, and the land where my garden lives. Your intentions could include what you want to focus on learning, a mindset that you want to cultivate while you are in your garden, or a set number of plants that you would like to grow. I suggest taking time out to think deeply about your intentions, clarify them, and then commit to them. Write your intentions down and put them in a place where you can see them. Remind yourself often of your intentions and re-commit to them if you get off track during the season.

In addition to the economic liberation from dispensaries that growing can provide, I hope that growing weed adds some joy to your life. One of the best experiences I have had in my adult life was doing spring garden prep on my farm for my second year of planting. I had one year of experience under my belt, so I had a clear vision of how I was going to do things better this second year. I was building raised beds, wheelbarrowing around soil, starting plants from seeds, all while listening to really fun electronic music on my iPod. I was regularly interrupting my "work" with wild dance breaks. I had tons of fun and really connected with my garden and my plants. Yes, I gardened mindfully in silence too but the dancing I did that spring was memorable. I hope that you too can grow in a way that brings fun and excitement into your life.

If you are unable to find joy in loving your plants, smoking their flowers, or sharing your bounty, you should probably stop growing. However, I do encourage you to at least give it a try.

This book is broken up into the basic elements of cultivation: The Plant Life Cycle, Soil, Sun, Water, Pests, Trellising, Harvest, and Hash Making. I encourage you to read through the entire book once to familiarize yourself with the process. Then you can use it as a guide as you move your way through the season. Also, these instructions come directly out of my experience cultivating cannabis in Humboldt County, California. I intentionally included instructions that may or may not be scientifically sound but are commonly practiced in the hills. I want this book to serve as both a guide for you and a cultural artifact for the community of people who taught me how to grow. This is what we did in those mountains. Now you can utilize the information that we developed and put it to work in your own garden. Enjoy, and have fun out there.

ABOUT ME

My first attempt at gardening was in Berkeley, California, where I was elected garden manager of the co-operative house where I lived, even though I had zero gardening experience. Clearly my community believed in my potential. I did, however, have interest and motivation to learn how to learn a practical skill. I was ready to try doing something with my hands and body as opposed to just using my mind. In order to learn, I took a student-led gardening class, then volunteered at Spiral Gardens, a local nonprofit nursery that grows fruiting and medicinal plants for the people. I fell so deeply in love with gardening that I quit school and moved to a Zen farm in rural Marin county, where I worked full-time in their garden. While there I also studied Zen Buddhism, which offered a unique perspective on horticulture. I came to understand gardening as an opportunity to develop my ability to pay attention. We worked in silence and were encouraged to pay attention to what it was that we were doing, while we did it. While I was forking soil, I was paying attention to forking the soil. If I was transplanting plants, all of my attention was paid to transplanting plants. I was encouraged to offer my life to each moment.

This is how I garden, except for when I occasionally bump music and shake my ass while carting around soil. I think it is all about balance.

After several years at this small Zen farm, I moved to a tiny mountain town in Humboldt County, where I found work in the cannabis industry as a trimmer. I lived in this town for five years and worked at nearly a dozen cannabis farms. I did every job available, from trimming to general labor to working as a harvest manager. I was blessed to have the opportunity to manage one of the extremely rare woman-owned farms in the area. I made sure to ask lots of questions everywhere I worked, as I always knew what a privilege it was to be learning how to grow from the men and women of Humboldt County. I was eventually fortunate enough to buy my own land and was able to start my own farm. Honestly, my mom bought me the property because she was worried about me living as a single woman in the Humboldt hills. Sexual harassment and assault on cannabis farms is common, and I had experienced my fair share of hassles. It was on my own farm, which I have affectionately named "Purple Kite Farm," that I was able to fuse the knowledge I had gained from Humboldt farmers with my belief in farming mindfully. This fusion resulted in a particular style of cannabis growing which I am very happy with. It is this particular style that I am sharing in these pages.

Last year I handed my farm over to friends, so that I could return to my hometown. However, my friends had never grown before, and it was my responsibility to teach them. I am very aware that I approach gardening from a unique perspective, and I wanted to share this with them. I ended up writing them a cultivation guide, which ultimately evolved into this book. To my greatest delight, my friends followed this guide closely and have become tremendously successful pot growers. With confidence and close study, I know that you will be tremendously successful too.

Part One

THE PLANT LIFE CYCLE

It is important to understand the life cycle of cannabis plants in order to appropriately care for them. Each stage of development presents a new set of challenges and opportunities for you to participate in their well-being. By understanding how the plants grow, and what they are capable of and when, you can maximize the efficacy of your support. It is essential for you to know what to expect at each stage and how to adequately care for your plants according to their developmental stage. Ultimately, the combination of strong, healthy genetics and appropriate care will result in the maturation of supremely healthy plants and the harvesting of beautiful, high quality flowers.

This approach to growing focuses on understanding the plants and how to care for them according to their developmental stage. This approach is cooperative, receptive, and requires you to pay close and careful attention.

This approach requires that you nurture your plants and respect their needs and their differences. If, ultimately, you learn anything from this book, it will be how to pay close attention to the unfolding of life and death. Your consciousness is part of this process! The closer and deeper the attention you can pay to your plants, the more gratifying your project will be. These plants will become your babies. You will experience the excitement of new beginnings, angst of sexual maturation, and the wistfulness of their final days. While any caretaking can feel like a stressful responsibility, there is nothing that provides the same sort of fulfillment and joy.

Does this all sound like hippie rhetoric? Well, considering that the best cannabis gardens have traditionally been grown by the hippies of Northern California, I certainly hope that it does.

The life of all cannabis plants starts with the sprouting of a seed. A seed grows into a male, female, or hermaphroditic plant with lots of leaves and branches. In order to prevent your plants from producing seeds (which you do not want), growers remove all male and hermaphroditic plants from their gardens, leaving only female plants. In mid–late July plants begin to transition from the "grow" phase into the "flower" phase. During the flower phase, the plants start to grow flowers that are harvested sometime around October. These flowers are hung to dry, trimmed, and then stored in an airtight container. In the pages that follow I will carefully lead you through each step.

GETTING STARTED

All cannabis gardeners will need to decide whether they will grow from seeds or clones (or both!). Seeds and clones both have their respective advantages and disadvantages.

Once this decision has been made, you will narrow in on what strains you will want to grow. Whether you decide to grow from seed or clone and whether you chose a sativa, indica, or hybrid strain will all tremendously impact your cultivation experience because these factors will largely determine the sensitivity of the plant, when it will be ready to harvest, the terpene profile (what it will smell and taste like), and (to some degree) what size it will be.

As a backyard grower, you are not held hostage by the demands of the market, and you get to have fun with growing in a way that most professional growers have long forgotten.

Clones and Seeds

Clones

A clone is a branch that was clipped off of another plant. The snipped branch is encouraged to grow roots through a special process and ultimately becomes a new plant with the exact same genetic makeup as the plant it came from. The original plant is known as the mother, and this new plant is the clone. One mother plant can make hundreds of clones.

Clones are wonderful because the plants are predictable and reliable. If you want to grow OG Kush and you grow out an OG Kush clone that you got from a trusted source, you can be nearly certain that the plant will produce the skunky, potent flowers that you desire. Also, there are many varieties, especially newer strains, that are only available for growing via clone. You can find clones at many dispensaries, and you can make your own clones once you have a plant with a well-established root system. When buying clones, make sure to check for healthy, white roots and leaves free of pest damage. Do not—I repeat, do not—bring home clones with any signs of pest damage. The very last thing you want to do at the start of the season is to introduce pests into your grow environment. Even if you are feeling desperate, just say no to sick and pest-covered clones. You will thank yourself later.

While clones are great for many reasons, the challenges are also diverse. Clones are more susceptible to pests and thus require an extremely vigilant and aggressive integrated pest management plan. Also, clones require supplemental light until you have over 14 ½ hours of daylight (or more). In 2018 in California, that day is May 26th. I suggest waiting to buy clones until after your region receives more than 14 ½ hours of daylight. You can find out when that day is in your region by looking for a daylight calculator online and putting in your city and state.

Seeds

Cannabis seeds are available for sale at many dispensaries. It is critical to do your homework to identify reputable seed companies that have seeds available in your area. The quality and reliability of seeds vary widely, so make sure to diligently research the companies that you are thinking about buying from. I suggest visiting your local dispensaries and making a list of seeds that you are interested in. Jot down the name of the strain and the seed company. Once you have a list, research each strain/seed company on the internet. Hopefully your search will lead to online forums where people have written reviews about that seed company and their respective strains. Another option is to attend a cannabis cup in your area. Seed companies often vend at these events and often have samples of flowers that come from each strain that they are selling. A final method of research is word of mouth. Ask your friends which seed companies that they have had good experiences with and which strains they have enjoyed growing out.

Growing from seed is great because the plants are fairly hardy, compared to clones, and typically grow more vigorously. Seeds can also be started in early spring without the use of supplemental light. Also, once you have your seeds, you can store them in a cool, dark place for months, if not years, until you are ready to plant. If you have more seeds than you need one year, you can save the remaining seeds for the following year.

There are several drawbacks to working with seeds. The first is that plants grown from seed will vary more than plants grown from clones. Depending on the seed company, some batches of seeds will vary more than others. One year a neighbor of mine grew out a dozen or so Tahoe OG Kush plants from seed. Sadly, among this dozen there were three phenotypes[3] that emerged, and he was sorely disappointed with two out of the three. This was a huge disappointment for him and a lifelong lesson for me. You cannot entirely rely on seeds to produce what they describe on their seed pack, especially if they are from a company that you are unfamiliar with. That said, most of my experience with seeds from companies that I trust have yielded plants that were mostly uniform and true to the strain description. In fact, the dankest weed I have ever grown was from seed. Sadly, those seeds were bred by a small company in Mendocino County and they were a limited release, so I was only able to grow out that strain for one season. In summary, seeds are more likely to yield surprises than clones, and if you are not comfortable with surprises, clones might be a preferable option for you.

The second drawback of working with seeds is that they will produce male and female plants, unless they are feminized. This is challenging because plants will take up to eight weeks after germination to show their sex. Once they do, you can dispose of the males. But until that time you will be caring for at least twice the amount of plants that you will eventually grow out. This takes up space and resources that you could otherwise give to plants that you will grow to maturity.

Ultimately, my preferred method is growing from feminized seeds from a reputable source. They are hardy, they do not need supplemental light, and I do not have to worry about sexing my plants. The major drawback of this method is that there are extreme limitations on the strains available in this form.

---

3 Phenotype is the observable characteristics of an organism. For cannabis this includes the color, smell, structure, and potency of the flowers.

Choosing a Strain

Once you have decided whether to grow from seed or from clone, you will then have to choose a strain. With hundreds of strains available to grow, you might find it difficult to decide which strains are right for you. I decide on strains according to flowering time, plant hardiness, terpene profile, yield, and availability of that strain in the form of a feminized seed.

First of all, the basics: Indicas are ready to be harvested early (September–October), sativas finish later (typically October–November), and hybrids are ready sometime in between. Indicas are known for having a relaxing, sedative "body high," whereas sativas have an energetic, cerebral "heady high." However, this designation between indicas as body high-inducing and sativas being heady high-inducing is strictly anecdotal and hotly debated. However, what I know to be true is that indicas typically stay short and stout with dense flowers, whereas sativas grow very tall and narrow with loose flowers.

Second, you will want to grow a strain that is either high in CBD (cannabidiol), THC (tetrahydrocannabinol), or a balance of the two. THC is the compound that weed is known for, which makes you high. CBD is a compound that has antioxidant, anti-inflammatory, anticonvulsant, antidepressant, antipsychotic, antitumoral, and neuroprotective qualities.[4] I suggest consulting the website projectcbd. org, which has a wealth of information about the therapeutic properties of CBD. While most farmers have traditionally chosen to grow plants high in THC, many farmers who are using their flowers medicinally are increasingly growing strains which have at least some CBD. Strains high in CBD include Sour Tsunami, Harlequin, and ACDC.

---

4 From Project CBD (projectcbd.org)

At my farm we are fortunate to have a fairly long growing season. However, I need to be certain that plants are finished by the end of October, or they will be destroyed by bad weather. That means that I cannot work with sativas or sativa-dominant hybrids that take longer than ten weeks to flower. While plants technically start flowering in July, my experience tells me that when a seed pack says that a plant will finish flowering and be ready for harvest in six weeks, that means six weeks or longer—after August 1st. This is approximate. The flowering time is calculated for plants growing indoors under controlled conditions. Your latitude will influence when your plants will start to switch into flowering. That said, I also believe that it is important to stagger the harvest so that plants ripen at different times, which allows harvest work to be spread out across the fall. At my farm we grow plants with a short flowering period (six weeks) and a few that have longer flowering periods (eight weeks). Flowering time is extremely important when it comes to which strains to choose because frost will kill your plants and harsh weather can damage your plants and their flowers. It is best to choose strains that will finish before your region experiences wet and cold conditions. You can do an internet search for when the first rains and/or frost date is for your zip code. You will want to start harvesting around the time of the first rains and have all of your plants harvested and drying by the time of the first frost.

The next factor to consider is your skill as a gardener. If you have grown cannabis for years and are reading this book as a refresher, or you are moving your indoor garden outside, then the entire world of strains is your oyster. However, for the novice grower, I suggest sticking with hybrid strains that are fairly insensitive to stress. I would recommend starting with a strain like Blue Dream, Trainwreck, or

Dream Queen, which have high stress tolerance. Once you have grown for a few seasons, then branch out to trickier strains.

Not only are some strains less sensitive to variations in watering and fertilizing, some plants seem to have a stronger immune system and are better at resisting pests and diseases. Usually seed packs and strain descriptions found online will tell you how hardy a particular strain is. In general, I would steer clear of designer strains such as Cookies, Gorilla Glue, and OG Kush on your first run. These strains tend to be less pest and disease resistant.

Finally, plant yield and the terpene profile of the flowers will factor into your decision. If you want a high-yielding plant, try G13. If you are looking for something with a sweet, floral terpene profile, I suggest trying something fruity like Sour Tangie or Pineapple Kush. I have noticed a very disheartening trend, which I want to make you aware of: skunky flowers have become far more popular in recent years because, I believe, they are perceived as more masculine. Sweet-smelling varieties, which are considered feminine, have become less desirable and even fetch a lower sales price. I beg you not to follow the skunk train and grow OG Kush and Headband because you heard that these strains are better. I guarantee that there are many wonderful strains out there, even sweet ones, which are potent and boast complex flavor profiles. Nothing against these grow-bro strains, but there are so many more to choose from.

With all of these considerations, the most important is your access to high quality seeds and clones. I am currently writing in Oakland, California, where access to seeds and clones is bountiful. If you do not live in an area where you have easy access to seeds and clones, I suggest planning a trip to the San Francisco Bay Area; Portland, Oregon; or Denver, Colorado, where many dispensaries keep a constant and diverse stock of seeds and clones. Many seeds are also available to order from the internet. If you choose that route, I suggest doing your homework to make sure that the company is reputable. Finally, seeds can be expensive. At the time of writing this book, most seeds are $10 to $40 each! Clones typically cost anywhere between $6 and $20.

Starting Seeds

Ideally you will start your seeds sometime between March and April, but I have started as late as July. I like to start in the middle of April because starting seeds earlier will make the resulting plants bigger. But if it is a long, wet spring, plants will be at an elevated risk for fungal disease and spring pest damage. If you desire small plants, start them late in the season. Ultimately you will need to assess your needs and limitations in regards to how big you want your plants to grow and how late your rainy season typically lasts.

I have successfully used many germination methods, so if you have a way of germinating that works for you, use that. Whether you follow my method or use your own, you will want to germinate seeds indoors and transplant them into pots outdoors. For germination you will need to clear a small amount of space near a window. When you transplant your germinated seeds into pots, you will want to do this step outside. Your plants will live outside after this point, ideally in a place that is both sunny and protected from strong winds. One method of germination that I really like, because you can keep your eyes on each seed, is sprouting them with the use of a slightly wet paper towel. The first step is to lightly moisten a paper towel and spread it out on top of a plate. An easy way to do this is to mist it with a spray bottle. Spread your seeds across the paper towel. Lay a second slightly wet paper towel on top of the seeds. Write the name of the seeds and the date on a plant tag with a pencil and set that somewhere on the plate where it is not in contact with any of the seeds. Set the plate next to a window and monitor the moisture levels of the paper towel. If it starts to dry out, spray it with a water bottle until remoistened. Seeds should germinate within 2–5 days.

Once your seeds have sprouted, write the name of the strain of each seed on separate plant tags with a pencil. Do not use a pen or permanent marker because the ink will quickly fade. Next, you will move your tags and seeds outside, where you will need a bag of organic potting soil and a 4-inch pot for each seed. You will fill each 4-inch pot to the brim with soil. Make sure the little holes on the bottom of the pot are wide open so that water can easily drain through them. For transplanting your sprouted seeds into pots, you will make a hole in the middle of the soil which is as deep as the width of the sprouted seed. This will be a tiny hole which you can make with the tip of a pencil. Gently place the germinated seed in the hole and cover it completely with a thin layer of soil. Be very gentle. Immediately stick the plant tag in the pot. Be extremely careful to use the right tag. I cannot overemphasize how important it is to keep seeds, seedlings, plants, etc. appropriately labeled. Pay attention, be careful, do not try to transplant a bunch and then tag later. Been there, done that, and it sucks to make these kinds of mix-ups. No shortcuts here. No spacing out.

Place all labeled 4 inch pots on plant heating pads if you have them. Any heating pad will do, but it needs to be connected to a reliable thermostat set around 68 degrees, which is the ideal soil temperature for seedlings. If you do not have heating pads, make sure that your seedlings are put in a place that receives lots of sunlight and minimal wind. Only use humidity domes in the case of frost threat. These domes encourage the accumulation of humidity and should be avoided if possible. Damping off, a deadly fungal infection, is a common problem during early stages of germination and growth which is a result of too much humidity and soil moisture. Pay close attention to the moisture levels of each pot and keep the soil warm. You are creating a nursery for these babies, and they need to be closely watched and pampered. Love them!

Slugs are also a common problem during this time, so preventative measures, such as sprinkling diatomaceous earth around warming tables and pots, should be taken to keep them away from seedlings. Diatomaceous earth can be found at most garden centers and pet supply stores.

Plants will continue to live in small pots for a few weeks. If your garden is not prepared for planting once the roots start to curl around the bottom of their pots, you will need to move your plants into 1-gallon pots. Your garden is ready for planting once the ambient air temperatures average in the high 60s and all of the soil in your beds is fertilized and free of weeds. This process of moving plants from small pots to larger pots is called transplanting. Transplant into larger pots once their roots have started to fill in the bottom of their pot. Use the same method for transplanting as you did with the seeds. However, from now on, every time you transplant make sure to do it in the shade to reduce shock to the plants. Fill a gallon pot full of fresh potting soil. I recommend using fresh potting soil, as opposed to reusing soil, in order to make sure that the soil is free of any pathogens that could harm the small plants. Make sure that there is at least ½ inch of free space between the top of the soil and the top of the pot. Fill the gallon pot with potting soil and remove soil from the top center of the pot, forming a hole that is just big enough to fit the root ball of the plant that you are transplanting. Remove the plant from the 4-inch pot and gently loosen its roots so that they no longer wind together into a tight mass. Gently place the plant into the hole and cover the roots with soil. Gently pat the soil into place around the plant. Water the plant thoroughly.

Once your plants have a few leaves, it is time to stake them. You will need a ⅛-inch bamboo pole and a small zip tie. You will plunge the bamboo stick into the soil until it hits the bottom of the pot. Use the zip tie to loosely connect the plant stalk and the bamboo stick. Make sure that the zip tie is loose enough for the plant to be able to continue to grow up through it. This stake will make sure that the plant is safe in case a super strong wind whips the plants around to the point of potentially snapping a stalk. This will also protect your plant in the case that something hits it, such as a swinging hose.

Sexing

At some point while the plants are in their teens (usually around eight weeks), they will "show their sex." Plants' sex organs grow in the node where a leaf grows from the main stem. Reproductive organs will sprout on both sides of the leaf, and both of them will either be male or female.

A male plant will sprout a ball with a tiny stem that looks like a crab claw. Eventually a cluster of balls will form and then drop. These are called panicles. If one of the balls opens, it will release pollen. If you find a male plant, kill it immediately. The only reason to ever keep a male is if you are trying to make seeds, but in your first year you will not be ready for that kind of project. A female plant will develop a small, tear-shaped pod without a stem, and it will have two white hairs, called stigmas, sticking out of it.

While most plants will show either male or female organs, some special plants will develop both. These plants are known as "herms," short for hermaphrodites, and they are important. If you mistake a herm for a female, the male flowers can release pollen, which can fertilize the female flowers. If female flowers are fertilized, the plants will put their energy into producing seeds rather than maturing resinous flowers. Cannabis flowers with seeds are known as "seeded" because they are full of seeds that you will have to pick out if you are trying to smoke any remaining flower. People claim that smoking seeds is a harsh experience and can cause headaches. It is imperative that you keep your eye out for herms and kill them when you find them. I know, this sounds like a true witch hunt, but you have to do it. To be clear, this is not some kind of horticultural manifestation of transphobia. It is simply a fact that if a male flower releases pollen, it will fertilize your female flowers and their quality will be degraded. I trust that you can love trans folks and everyone else on the gender spectrum while simultaneously removing all male and herm plants from your garden.

Plants can herm at any point during the season in response to stressful conditions. It is necessary to check for male parts throughout the season. Do not let your guard down with this issue. Keep a close eye on the sex of every part of all plants (herms can be all female except for a single male branch! Sneaky!) I cannot emphasize how important it is to pay close attention to this. Also, if any of your neighbors are growing, they will be really, really, really mad because the pollen could seed their plants too. This has happened in my neighborhood before, and it was baaaddddd.

Preparing to Plant

Before you plant, these tasks must be completed:

• The soil is around 68 degrees and NOT sopping wet from rain.

• Plants have hardened off for 2 weeks.

• Irrigation system is in working order.

• All holes/pots/beds are amended and weeded.

• All plants must be free of pests.

It is time to transplant into your garden when the soil reaches 68 degrees. The easiest way to assess soil temps is with daytime temps in your area. If the weather in your area is averaging in the high 60s, your soil will be warm enough to plant. The reason for waiting until soil warms up is because beneficial bacteria become active in warmer temperatures. The problem with planting too early can be frost damage, slug damage, and fungal infections. I recommend getting everything ready for planting as early as possible so that as soon as temps start to rise you will be ready to get plants into the ground.

Before planting out, make sure the plants "harden off." Hardening off is a process of acclimating plants grown indoors or in greenhouses to the increased intensity of light and wind that they will experience living outdoors. If your starts have been living outside since birth, you do not need to worry about hardening them off. When plants are grown indoors or in greenhouses, their leaves are delicate, like baby skin, and the stalk is weak. When plants are grown outdoors, they start off fragile but quickly toughen up. Plants grown indoors or in greenhouses need time to acclimate to the stress of wind and direct sunlight. Plants should be given 7–10 days to gradually adjust to the rougher and more intense conditions of the outdoors before being set outside to live. Do this by setting them outside in the early morning or evening on a day when there is not very much wind or heat. Each day until planting, increase the amount of time plants spend outside and introduce them to more light and windy conditions. This process will reduce the amount of shock that your plants will encounter when moving out of their comfortable, climate-controlled space inside to the intense conditions of the garden. Your plants will not look noticeably different, but they are much less likely to be stunted or killed by the stress of moving plants from indoor conditions to outdoors.

Planting

Planting is pretty straightforward. Make a hole in the top of the soil, large enough to fit the root ball of the plant. Turn the pot of the plant upside down to extract the plant from its pot with all of its soil. Gently loosen the plant's roots so that they don't continue to spiral around each other. Set the root ball into the hole, cover up the hole with soil, pat the soil firmly in place and water the plant until the soil is sopping wet. Keep the plant with its supporting bamboo stake and plant tag. You will remove the stake later, once you add a layer of trellising, but for now just keep it with its support stick. Once everything is planted, water each plant in deeply and turn on your automatic irrigation system (this will be discussed in the water chapter). Schedule it to start watering the following day.

Preparing for Flowering

Plants begin their transition into flowering in early July, but you might not see changes until the beginning of August. It is important to start feeding your plants a balanced fertilizer that is high in phosphorous in mid-July to give it time to break down in the soil and for nutrients to become available by the time the plants need it. I will discuss fertilizers in depth in a later chapter.

Late July/early August is a critical period for plants. They are going through a dramatic transformation from a period of vegetative growth (vegging) to a period of floral growth (flowering), and this stress compromises their immune systems. At this point you want to treat the plants like they are pregnant, because they are! Sort of. Robust and healthy mamas are more likely to make it through pregnancy with their health intact and with healthy babies. With plants, all of this applies. Pests and pathogens will begin to proliferate at this time, especially if plants are stressed by nutrient deficiency or insufficient watering. It is very important to boost plant health during this critical period with the following measures:

- Make absolutely certain that plants are well watered and that there is never any water stress. Overwatering at this point is better than underwatering.
- Make sure that there are zero signs of nutrient deficiencies. If you spot any, make sure to thoroughly fertilize. I give detailed instructions on how to fertilize in a later chapter.
- Do a very careful walk-through of the garden in mid and late July. Look closely for the presence of any pests. If any are present, spray all plants with the appropriate organic pesticides. Spray as directed. From this point on continue to pay close attention to the presence of pests. Address problems immediately and aggressively. I will discuss pest management in more detail in a later chapter.
- Look closely for male and/or hermed plants and immediately remove any and all of these from your garden.

If you see any signs of pests on one plant, take a slow and close look at all of your plants. You might be very surprised by how many plants are actually showing signs of this same pest. Take pest presence extremely seriously. Spray every plant, with organic pesticides, that is showing signs of pest damage.

August is a time of flower maturation. Plants will go into full flowering and their branches will become heavy. It is essential that all of your systems that you have put in place—irrigation, trellising, and pest management—are up and running. Make sure that plants are well fertilized, well watered, and that all pests are under control. Days are growing shorter in August, and you might begin to have a few cool evenings. Cool, damp evenings can foster mildew development, and so make sure to monitor for powdery mildew. If an early rain hits, you will also need to begin monitoring for grey mold. If there is any way that you can cover your plants and prevent them from being rained on, I highly encourage this. Pop-up carports and canopies work well, and you can typically find used ones on Craigslist. New canopies can be found at Costco and on eBay. Just make sure that you remove the cover after the rains and that any cover still allows plants to have sufficient airflow through their canopy.

I will thoroughly address harvest procedures later in this text. Once all flowers have been removed from the garden, you can remove the trellising, chop back large branches, and pull the stalk out of the ground. If you have access to a chipper, run the plant through a chipper and use the chips for garden mulch. If you do not have a chipper, chop the plant up into small pieces and compost.

Part Two

CREATING A GOOD GROWING ENVIRONMENT

My formative gardening teacher was a Zen Buddhist monk who was the garden manager of the land where I was doing work practice. She was intelligent, strong, very organized, and had a great eye for beauty. Every day before work she would lead a short Buddhist prayer as one of the garden crew members lit incense and led a series of bows to Kuan Yin, the Buddhist goddess of compassion. My work with this teacher inspired within me the belief that gardening was a practice of dharma, or the unity of wisdom and compassion. It requires great wisdom to understand the seasonal cycles of the earth, how those cycles affect plants in general, and the specific needs of each plant. It takes compassion to tend to each plant according to their unique needs in order for them to flourish.

My formative cannabis cultivation teacher was a young mountain woman with a spicy personality. She hired me one season to manage her harvest, so that she could focus her energy on activism related to indigenous water rights. She was a badass. She worked closely with me, so that I understood every step of the cultivation and harvest process. During harvest, I was empowered to run her farm while she was away at conferences and work. I did not feel prepared for such responsibility, but I took what she had taught me and did the best that I could. Without that experience of making all of the big decisions, I do not think I ever would have started my own farm. I felt like this woman passed on the cannabis farming baton to me, and I am now passing it on to you. The skills that you need to cultivate might feel overwhelming, but I believe in you just like my two gardening teachers believed in me.

In order to grow cannabis successfully, you will need to develop a basic understanding of the cannabis life cycle and the unique needs of cannabis plants. While I have written this guide for those of you who have never worked with plants, the amount of information that you will need to familiarize yourself with, still might feel daunting. If at any point you feel like there is just too much to learn, close the book and take care of yourself. Meditate, take a walk, call a friend. Relieve yourself of any and all anxiety related to learning this brand new subject and return to the material once you have relaxed and are ready to take another bite. You are entirely capable of learning this material and cultivating the foundational wisdom required to take care of your plants.

WHERE TO PLANT

In order to grow weed you will need to either have the decision-making power over what happens on the land where you live, or you need to obtain consent from the other people who hold that decision-making power. When I lived in Humboldt, I would guess that 2% of the land was owned by women, and so it was hardly a surprise that so few women grew weed relative to the men who grew. It is clear to me that this gender disparity in land ownership has directly led to the male domination of the cannabis industry and dismally small number of women cultivators. Sadly, there is no quick and easy solution to the disparity of land ownership between men and women in this country. F*$% that.

Exhale.

Assuming you do have access to a backyard, a rooftop, or a deck where you can grow, it is important that it is super sunny and protected from strong winds and large animals. Also, your garden should be as private as possible because for now and into the near future, cannabis is very valuable, and folks desperate for a little extra cash or smoke might be tempted to steal your plants if they see them.

Site Selection

Every outdoor cannabis cultivator needs space to grow. However, not all outdoor space is equal. If possible, select a site that is south-facing and free of tall barriers such as trees and walls that will block sunlight. This can be in your backyard, on a terrace, a deck, or even a rooftop. A site that is south-facing and clear of barriers will ensure the most possible sunlight exposure for your plants. In addition to south facing you will need easy access to water. You will need to be able to access your plants with a hose, and this requires having a spigot close to your garden area. I strongly advise against hand watering with a watering can throughout the season because of how labor-intensive and time-consuming this would be. However, if there is absolutely no way for you to plant close to a spigot or a faucet, this is your only other option.

You also want a site that is safe from thieves. In some neighborhoods, you will need to make sure that your plants are behind a locked, tall fence. In other neighborhoods where growing is common and your neighbors are friendly to the practice, it might be OK for your plants to be visible. You will need to carefully determine how much privacy you will need to feel comfortable and plan accordingly. Many backyard growers rely on bamboo fencing lined with landscaping fabric to create walls that hide their plants from neighbors and guests. Some growers choose sites in their yard that are hidden by greenhouses, sheds, and other small structures. It is essential to determine the privacy needs for your site before you begin working. Plants grow quickly, and it is better to build your fences and erect your privacy screens before the garden work begins.

In addition to finding a site that is private, you will also need it to be free of pests. Make sure that your grow site is well fenced if your backyard attracts deer or bears. I strongly encourage you to plant in pots if there is a gopher presence in your area. Dogs, cats, rats, squirrels, raccoons, etc. can also cause problems in gardens by accidentally breaking branches that are not well trellised. I suggest creating barriers that will keep all animals out of your garden, if possible.

Finally, if you are planning on growing your cannabis in the ground, choose a site where the native soil is amenable to gardening. Rocky, compacted, or sandy soils are not ideal for cannabis cultivation. If you have any indication that the soil you would like to grow in has been polluted, make sure to get your soil tested. If it is polluted, do not plant your cannabis in the ground.

You will want to dig holes 18–25 inches deep and with a diameter of roughly 5 feet or your desired canopy size. Generally speaking, the deeper and wider your holes are, the larger your plants will be.

Container Planting

An easy and popular alternative to cultivating cannabis in the ground is cultivating it in containers. In fact, most cannabis farmers in the Emerald Triangle grow cannabis this way. Growing in large pots allows farmers to have the most control over the soil conditions of their plants. While growing in pots full of bagged soil trucked into your garden center from who knows where is certainly not the environmentally friendly option, it is extremely easy and will keep your plants safe from gophers. Bagged soil uses tons of plastic and relies on trucking, which uses enormous amounts of fossil fuels to get organic soil to you. It is hard to justify using it, but it does simplify the soil preparation process.

If you decide that you would like to grow using containers, I suggest using "fabric pots," which are cheap, easy to work with, and last for several seasons. Fabric pots are typically made out of a thick landscaping fabric that feels like felt. Fabric pots also "air prune" roots, which prevents plants from becoming root-bound. Typically, when a plant is grown in a container, the roots will grow in a coil, and over time this coil will become very dense. This is known as becoming root-bound. Once a dense mass of roots is established, a plant will start to show symptoms of being root-bound, which include stunted growth, wilting, diminished flower growth, and stretching. However, with a fabric pot, the roots that grow against the sides of the pot will stop growing but will continue to take in water and nutrients. This process is known as air pruning, and it prevents plants from becoming root-bound. An alternative to fabric pots, which can be more expensive but also more aesthetically appealing, are tree planters. They can be found at garden centers and online. Tree planters are pots that are large enough to grow trees, and they are available in materials including black plastic, redwood, ceramic, and steel. Whatever material you choose, make sure that your container has sufficient drainage.

An additional method of container planting to consider is the use of raised beds. When I bought my property, there was an old chicken coop which I dismantled and used the lumber to build raised beds. I used the 2x4s to build the frames for the beds and lined them with burlap. This method was very inexpensive, allowed the roots to "air prune," and I was able to fit lots of plants into a smaller space because there was no gap between plant containers. If you do not have materials that you can repurpose into a raised bed, I suggest using materials that are less prone to rot, such as cedar or redwood. However, these rot-resistant types of wood are expensive. You can line your beds with wood, but do not use pressure treated wood or plywood, both of which are soaked with toxic chemicals and glues.

Plant Spacing

When designing your garden you will have to figure out how far apart to plant each plant. There are two general methods. There is the traditional outdoor method of giving each plant as much room as possible on all sides. I have heard about growers planting their plants 4 to 12 feet apart, depending on how large they anticipate their plants to grow. For a Blue Dream plant started from seed in the spring in a Mediterranean climate, I suggest planting with at least 7 feet between each plant stalk. This will enable maximum airflow and sun exposure for each plant. If you have more room, feel free to space them farther apart. Generous spacing between plants makes it easier for you to move between plants, which is especially helpful when looking for pests and hermed branches.

The second method comes from indoor growing, where space is usually very limited. It is known as Sea of Green, a.k.a. the SOG method. With the SOG method, you plant lots of plants close together and use Hortonova trellising (I will discuss this later) to space out the canopy so that you create a hedge of cannabis. As the plants grow, they intertwine, and you will treat them as if they are one big organism. This method is good if your space is limited;

however, the more densely you plant, the more difficult it is to detect and address problems.

Honestly, if you have lots of plants and a little amount of space, I recommend growing with a SOG method. If you have tons of space and not very many plants, I recommend generously spacing your plants. If you are really experimental, you can try both and see which method works better for you. I strongly recommend experimentation.

NUTRIENTS

Fertilizing can be a very simple process. You can buy premixed nutrients and feed your plants with the help of a fertigator, which is a device that slowly adds nutrients into your irrigation water. In this book, we are going to keep the fertilization process extremely simple. I have simplified it into fertilizing with "grow" while the plant is growing branches and leaves, and switching to "bloom" when the plant begins to produce flowers.

I am a big advocate of the K.I.S.S. (Keep It Simple Smarty) method of fertilizing. I will not use this as an opportunity to rant about the grow store owners and fertilizer companies that push crazy amounts of unnecessary fertilizers on growers. I will simply say that cannabis is a flower. Like all flowers, it needs a balanced fertilizer high in nitrogen for the first half of its life and a balanced fertilizer high in phosphorous for the second half of its life. By balanced, I mean that it has some amount of nitrogen, phosphorous, potassium (N-P-K), and trace minerals but higher amounts of nitrogen during the veg stage and higher amounts of phosphorus during flowering. Generally speaking, nitrogen helps with overall plant growth, phosphorous helps with floral development, and potassium helps with healthy root growth and overall plant health.

When deciding which fertilizer to use, I suggest keeping a few key variables in mind. The first variable is whether or not the amendment is organic. Organic amendments generally sourced from plant and/or animal sources quickly decompose over the course of the season. Organic fertilizers are free of synthetic chemicals and genetically modified material. Organic amendments include chicken poop, kelp meal, oyster shell, and bone meal. Some growers choose to only use vegan, organic (veganic) inputs, which I think is amazingly-wonderfully-compassionate. If you look around the internet you can find premixed organic and veganic fertilizer mixes, but as of the writing of this text, there are no liquid, veganic, premixed fertilizers. The next variable is whether to use a water soluble or liquid fertilizer. The water-soluble fertilizer will dissolve in water and is generally cheaper. The liquid fertilizer is generally more expensive but is more readily available in garden centers.

The final variable is whether or not to mix your own balanced fertilizer or to buy it premixed. Throughout the season your plants are going to need a healthy supply of nitrogen (N), phosphorus (P), and potassium (K). During the grow phase your plants will need more nitrogen, and during their flower phase plants will need more phosphorous. I strongly suggest buying premixed fertilizers, one that is high in nitrogen and a second that is high in phosphorous. Trying to figure out the correct balance of N-P-K is far too anxiety-inducing for a first-time grower. The advantage to mixing your own is the cost. However, in my opinion, the ease of using a premixed fertilizer far outweighs the price difference.

Getting Started with Fertilizer

To get started, make a simple fertilizer log where you can keep track of when you applied fertilizer, which fertilizers were used, and at what rate. Keep this log going all season. Trust me, when the season picks up, you will not be able to remember if the last feeding was five days or two weeks ago. This log will save you from having to recall these sorts of fine details.

Equipment you will need for fertilizing plants includes: a hose, a watering wand, and a fertigator. I recommend buying a nice watering wand because you will be using it a lot, and a cheap wand can turn watering into a frustrating activity. A fertigator is a plastic jug that you can fill with water-soluble fertilizer. With the use of special tubes and nozzles, it will release fertilizer slowly through your drip irrigation lines.

You do not need to shop for your fertilizer at a cannabis grow store to get your hands on effective fertilizers that will keep your plants healthy. In fact, I would suggest steering clear of these places, because you will almost certainly spend more than necessary and leave with stuff that you do not need. I suggest visiting your local garden center or looking online for an organic, balanced, liquid fertilizer. You will need one which is high in nitrogen and one which is high in phosphorus. A few brands that I am familiar with are Peaceful Valley, Biolink, G&B Organics, and Dr. Earth. When looking for fertilizer, make sure that it is organic, in liquid or water-soluble form, and includes all three major nutrients: nitrogen, phosphorous, and potassium. You will want one fertilizer blend which is high in nitrogen relative to the other nutrients and one that is high in phosphorous relative to the other nutrients. I do not recommend newbie growers blending your own nutrients, but this is definitely something to explore as you become more familiar with growing and the needs of your plants.

Preparing Your Soil

My simple recommendation is this: fill your pots or raised beds with organic potting soil. If you can find a potting soil that uses coconut fiber (a.k.a. coco peat) instead of peat moss, that would be great. Peat bogs are endangered and we need to stop mining them for peat. If you are using potting soil, check to make sure that it is amended with nutrients. If it is not amended, or you are using potting soil that that has been used for a season or more already, or you are planting in the ground, you can amend it with an all-purpose, organic, dry fertilizer and compost. Follow the application directions on the bags of compost and fertilizer. I suggest amending your soil a few weeks before you plant so that the bacteria in the soil have time to start breaking down the nutrients in the soil and making them available to your plants.

FERTILIZING STARTS

After 2 to 3 weeks of growth, it is time to start fertilizing your plants with liquid nutrients. If the deep green of the plant leaves begins to fade or lower leaves start yellowing, it is definitely time to feed. Simply follow the instructions indicated on the fertilizer container. During this early stage, you will want to stay ahead of your plants. You do not want their vibrant green to fade to yellow; however, you also do not want to burn the plants with too much nitrogen. You will need to pay close attention to how plants respond to feedings and flush them immediately with lots of water if they show signs of nutrient burn. Nutrient burn is when a plant takes in more nutrients than it can use. This can cause the tips of the leaves to turn yellow. Flushing will not reverse the burn, but it will flush excess fertilizer that could result in further damage. If you do discover burned leaves and/or leaf tips, just leave them alone. If you choose to use a fertilizer with synthetic chemicals, you will need to be especially vigilant not to burn your plants with too much fertilizer.

Cannabis plants are extremely heavy feeders, and you will need to be vigilant in your feedings. I suggest keeping your eyes on the lower leaves, or the skirt. If these leaves are bright green, you are fertilizing enough. If they start to lighten and turn yellow, the plant needs more nitrogen rich fertilizer. If the skirt turns dark green and the tips turn yellow, you have overfertilized. Finding the sweet spot is difficult and will be different for each strain. As plants grow, their need for fertilizer shifts. Experiment and know that there is no "correct" feeding schedule or amount, just as there is no correct feeding interval or amount that you can use for all people. You will need to get to know your plants well and try to meet the needs that they are indicating with their lower leaves.

Some people treat their cannabis plants like pigs that they are raising for slaughter. They feed them massive amounts of fertilizer to grow the biggest plants possible. I will admit, I have used this method before; however, I do not recommend it. Overfertilizing can cause a host of problems. If you are concerned about yields, I suggest growing two or three small plants instead of one extremely large one, grow from seed, choose strains which are known to be heavy yielders, or start your plants in the winter under lights.

How to Feed

Feeding your plants with a fertigator is easy. While plants are still in pots, connect your fertigator to the spigot and connect your hose to the fertigator. Set the fertigator on low. Fill your fertigator up with a water-soluble or liquid, high-nitrogen fertilizer. Water your plants as you normally would. A small amount of fertilizer will be mixed into the water, and every time you water your plants you will also be fertilizing them. Once your plants are in radiant health, you can disconnect the fertigator. If your plants start to fade in color again while they are still in pots, reconnect the fertigator. Once plants are planted out into the garden and the drip system is established, connect the fertigator to the drip system. Fill the jug every 7 to 14 days. Gradually transition from a high-nitrogen fertilizer to a high-phosphorous fertilizer towards the end of July.

An alternative method of feeding which does not require using a fertigator is buying an organic or veganic premixed dry fertilizer that you can scratch into your soil. These fertilizers are slower acting and are more labor-intensive to apply. I recommend that you check the feeding instructions on the fertilizer box or bag to determine how much to use and how often. You will need to buy two different kinds of fertilizer mixes: one for the grow period and one for the flower period.

Nutrient Deficiencies and Toxicity

A common problem for most gardens are over- or under-fertilizing. Plants need a wide array of nutrients, in optimal amounts, for them to thrive. We have discussed the needs for the macronutrients of phosphorous, potassium, and nitrogen. Plants also need zinc, iron, boron, magnesium, calcium, and a long list of minerals. If a plant is starved of macro- or micronutrients, it will show signs of deficiencies. If the plant has been overfed with any of these nutrients, the plant will show signs of toxicity. Nitrogen is the most important nutrient which will show obvious signs of toxicity or deficiency. A plant that is nitrogen deficient will develop yellow leaves from the bottom up, and its growth will slow to a crawl. A plant suffering from nitrogen toxicity will develop deep green leaves, tips will turn in, and sometimes the leaf tips will die back and turn yellow or brown. A plant suffering from nitrogen toxicity will increase its vulnerability to pests and disease. If you have a plant that is suffering from nitrogen deficiency, gradually increase how much nitrogen you supply your plant during each feeding until green coloring has returned to the entire plant. Leaves that have yellowed will die and drop off, but all new growth should be bright green. In the case of toxicity, reduce the amount of nitrogen that you are adding to feedings until your plant lightens in color. Addressing nutrient deficiencies and toxicities can feel very confusing and overwhelming because there are so many nutrients to address and so many signs of nutrient imbalance that can appear. I suggest that during your first year you limit your concern to nitrogen, and over time, as you expand your knowledge base about growing cannabis, you can dig deeper into this aspect of cultivation. There are many internet forums where cultivators discuss nutrient deficiencies and help other cultivators identify and address problems. These forums are a great place to connect with other cultivators while expanding your knowledge of one of the more complicated aspects of cannabis cultivation.

Mulching

Many gardeners choose to mulch their gardens once they have planted to retain soil moisture. While I understand this is the responsible thing to do, I generally do not suggest it. I know this makes me a bad person, but I have my reasons. If this shocks and disgusts you, just mulch and skip this section.

I am not a fan of mulching for two reasons: it is difficult to see if there are problems with the irrigation system, and it makes it difficult to see if there is anything weird happening with the soil. One year I pulled back the mulch to discover that the dry amendments that I had used had not been mixed into the soil well enough and they were molding on top of the soil! Another time I peeled back the mulch to discover a million potato bugs. Another time I peeled back the mulch only to realize that the soil was bone dry. The lines had been clogged and the plant had not been receiving water for I do not know how long. So for me, mulching means surprises, and I do not like surprises when I'm cultivating cannabis. Mulching is good for keeping moisture in the soil and keeping plant roots cooler, but in my opinion, the bad outweighs the good. Irrigation lines do burst and/or fall out of place. Lines also clog, leaving plants that you thought were getting plenty of water without any. If there is mulch hiding the lines, you won't be able to quickly identify such problems. In time, plants will become large enough to shade the soil under their canopy and help cool soil temps.

SUN

Cannabis requires lots of sunlight in order to stay healthy, grow large, and produce dense, terpene-rich flowers. While the study of light is especially useful for indoor growers, there are a few basic ideas about light that are also helpful for outdoor growers.

First let us start with the basics of photosynthesis. This is the process whereby a plant takes in sunlight, which synthesizes carbon dioxide and water to create sugar and oxygen. The plant releases the oxygen and uses the sugar to grow. This feels deeply miraculous to me.

Growers usually refer to fertilizers as plant food because they help to boost plant growth, but in truth, there is no greater plant food than carbohydrates created with the help of sunlight. No matter how much fertilizer you give a plant, it will not grow if it does not have sufficient exposure to high intensity light.

Ideally you want your plants exposed to the equivalent of midday, midsummer sunlight for as many days as possible. Midday, midsummer light is the highest intensity light that your plants will be exposed to during the season. Photosynthesis and growth are accelerated at this time, when light is the most intense. This is why it is important to wait until spring has sprung in your area before starting your seeds. Sprouting them before light intensity has started to increase, when days are still fairly dark and cloud cover is common, will result in plants sitting in their pots and not putting on much growth. Photosynthesis is happening very slowly in this low light condition.

If the soil and growing conditions are damp, this scenario will inevitably lead to the development of fungal diseases. This is also why you want to choose a strain that finishes while there is still strong light intensity in your area. In the mountains of Humboldt County you want a strain that finishes in early October, which is when both the light intensity noticeably weakens and the first rains arrive. Because of the decreased light intensity, flowers that continue to develop after this time lack the density that most growers desire.

There are a few times during the season when low light intensity is desirable. Delicate young plants that have been raised indoors or in a greenhouse cannot be exposed to intense light. It is important to acclimate these plants to intense light. First, expose them to direct morning and evening light, which is generally too weak to burn plants. You will know that your plants are experiencing light burn if you see leaves that look bleached. Gradually increase their exposure to intense light until they are ready to grow underneath the full force of midday sun. Also, you need low light intensity when transplanting. I generally transplant in the shade or on a cloudy day. This reduces the risk of plant stress, otherwise known as transplant shock.

For the most part, exposure to lower intensity light for prolonged periods is not ideal. It will slow the growth of your plants. Also, plants that take an extended period to flower and are ripening in the fall, when the light has lost much of its intensity, will produce flowers that are loose in structure, aka "larfy." Larfy buds smoke just fine, but they do not have the same visual appeal as dense flowers. They are also more difficult to trim.

WATER

When it comes to cannabis, water is very important. Plants cannot access nutrients without moisture. They also need moisture as part of the evaporation process that cools plants off on hot days. Continuously keeping soil moist is very important.

However, determining how much water to give to your plants can be confusing and feel overwhelming. To be honest, after years of growing I still cannot pinpoint exactly how much each plant needs at every stage of its life. However, I do have a few guidelines that I use to figure out when and how much to water my plants.

Soil is a Sponge

First, let us start with a visualization exercise. Think about a sponge. A real sponge. Imagine it. Seriously. Now imagine completely soaking it by placing it under a faucet for a few minutes. See it? Now, let us go through a few scenarios:

1. **Imagine turning the faucet back on for a few minutes with the sponge still sitting underneath it. What happens? Does the sponge become even more wet? Does it stay wetter longer?**

The answer to all of these questions is no. Once the sponge is at its capacity for water absorption, that is it. The amount of water a particular soil can absorb is technically known as its field capacity. Once at field capacity, the sponge (or soil) cannot and will not become wetter. The water in the sponge is simply displaced by the additional water poured onto the sponge.

So, once soil is soaked thoroughly, you can stop watering it. During the summer when plants are in the ground or in large pots, the water will need to reach at least 12 inches deep. Once water has reached this depth, your plants do not need more water. Once a pot or a hole has reached this point, it is at 'field capacity' and it is time to stop watering. Seriously, beyond that point it is simply a waste of water.

The goal is not to have sopping wet soil. There is a range of acceptable moisture levels. The range is *not* sopping wet to bone dry. The ideal range is from wet (like a sponge that just cleaned up a spilled glass of water) to delicately moist (almost dry but with a sheen). The soil that touches roots should never look dull: at that point it is completely dry and will need to be thoroughly saturated with water in order to rehydrate it.

2. What happens if you let the sponge completely dry out and try to soak it again? Will it be more difficult to make the entire sponge wet again? Will the water bead off of the surface or immediately soak in?

Just like a sponge, soil will have a very difficult time taking in water once it has completely dried out. Not only will the top crust cause water to bead off and flow down and out the sides of a pot or a bed, once it does begin to penetrate the soil there will be dry pockets that will be difficult to remoisten.

The best solution to this problem is to not let the soil become so dry. If a crust develops, break it up with your hands and check to make sure that lower layers are getting wet and that there are no dry pockets left. Dry pockets can linger even when other parts of a pot are sopping wet, if they are not physically broken apart. Make sure that you are thorough when looking for them. Also, if a pot of soil does become bone dry, make sure to give it lots of water and check to make sure that the soil at the bottom of the pot/bed is moist before you stop watering. It is common that the top part of the soil becomes remoistened while the bottom remains dry. If you notice that this is happening with your soil, you will need to thoroughly saturate your plants with water and break apart dry pockets with your hands, if possible.

3. What is the ideal wetness of the sponge/soil?

There will be a range from wet at the time of watering to delicately moist right before plants need to be watered. Ultimately it is the job of the gardener to closely monitor soil conditions and set watering schedules according to evaporation rates.

Heat and wind will accelerate the drying process, especially exposed areas. Make sure to vigilantly check moisture levels, especially during hot, dry, and windy conditions, and compensate with additional water.

4. **What happens if the sponge remains soaked for prolonged periods? Will it start to smell like mildew, a.k.a. have fungal problems?**

Yes! A sponge that sits in the sink and remains sopping wet quickly grows mildew, especially in warm climates. Similarly, roots that sit in warm, sopping wet soil will likely develop damping off or root rot. Proper drainage and appropriate watering practices are essential methods for preventing fungal infections.

Drenching the soil is OK as long as the water drains efficiently and the soil does not remain drenched for prolonged periods. Let the soil dry out, let oxygen in, let the soil breathe, then water again before the soil becomes too dry. Remember, it is a cycle from wet to delicately moist.

Roots need water, but they also need oxygen. Soil that is constantly waterlogged will not contain an ideal amount of oxygen, and this can stress your plants.

The ideal moisture level of soil is that of a thoroughly wrung out sponge. This requires that the soil has good drainage and that evaporation conditions are ideal. Ambient humidity must be low in order for the plant to draw moisture from the roots to the tips of the plant. Be cautious not to overwater. This can easily happen if you follow a routine watering schedule regardless of weather conditions and plant size. On cool, overcast days, when low temps

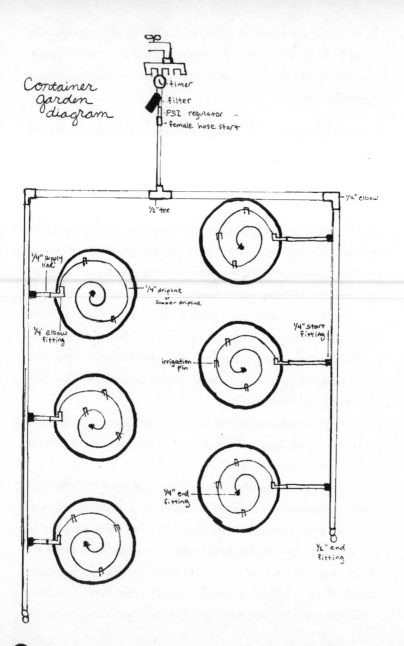

Container
garden
diagram

- timer
- filter
- PSI regulator
- female hose start

½" tee

½" elbow

¼" supply line

¼" dripline
or
soaker dripline

¼" elbow fitting

¼" start fitting

irrigation pin

¼" end fitting

½" end fitting

and high humidity slow down evaporation, plants will not need to be watered as often as when it is dry, hot, and windy out.

When plants are small, they will not need nearly as much water as when they are large. This is the same as taking care of a child or a pet; when they are small, they need less water. If it is hot out and they are sweating (transpiring), they need more water.

As the season progresses, you will need to increase your watering, and as fall approaches, you can decrease watering significantly. It is incredibly important to scale down watering once cool weather returns because your plants will be vulnerable to developing root rot, which can kill your plants. Make sure that the soil is cycling between wet and lightly moist.

Finally, be aware of underwatering. Plants need oxygen but they also need water. On hot, windy days, when plants are growing quickly and their root systems are filling up their pots, they might need to be watered twice. If this is happening regularly, it is time to move plants into larger pots. Underwatering not only inhibits growth, it can stress plants and weaken their immune system, thus making them susceptible to pathogens. If the soil of some plants is drying out much quicker than others, adjust the conditions to match those of the rest of the plants. Avoid putting plants in locations where the sides of their pots receive direct sunlight for extended periods. Plants do not respond well when their roots are heated above 85 degrees. This can happen easily with plants grown in containers.

Irrigation

I start my plants in 4-inch pots and transplant them into gallon pots after 4 to 6 weeks of growth. I move plants into larger containers once their roots begin to circle around the bottom of their pot. During

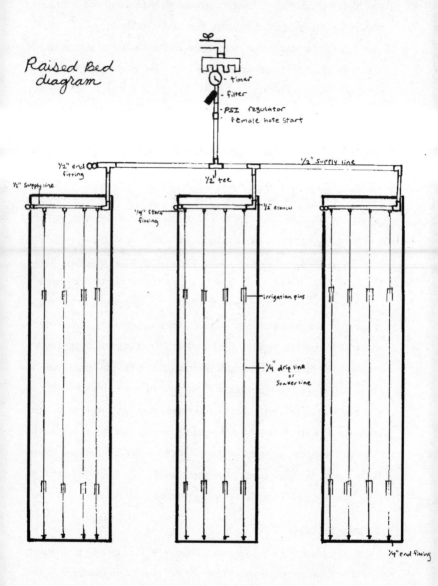

Raised Bed
diagram

- timer
- filter
- PSI regulator
- female hose start

½" end fitting

½" Supply line

½" Supply line

½" tee

½" elbow

¼" Start fitting

irrigation pins

¼" drip line
or
Soaker line

¼" end fitting

March, April, and into May, while my plants are still in small pots, I hand water them either with a watering can or with a hose with a watering wand attached. However, once I transplant them into their final homes—either in the ground, in raised beds, or in large fabric pots—I rely on an automated drip system to keep my plants watered.

If you are not ready to invest in an automated irrigation system, you can hand water your plants every 3–5 days. You will need to water each plant deeply. That said, I strongly suggest setting up a drip system as soon as your finances allow. This empowers you with the freedom to take weekend trips to the beach and to go to festivals without worrying about who is going to water your babies. It also saves you an enormous amount of time. Watering a few large plants a few times a week can take hours, depending on weather conditions and the size of the plants.

On preceding pages are two diagrams of drip systems with a list of all of their components.

Drip systems are easy to install and save you enormous amounts of time and energy throughout the season. Drip systems are like Legos or tinker toys. You buy an assortment of parts and put them together to create a plumbing system. The best resource for learning more about drip systems is by going to the Drip Works website (dripworks.com), and they can guide you through the process of designing a system and selecting parts.

An important part of setting up an automatic drip system is setting the timers. I recommend starting with 30 minutes of water every other morning. This is good for roots that are still small and close to the soil's surface. Also, you are not yet dealing with too much summer heat. As roots grow and temps swell, increase your watering time. You will need to experiment to see how deeply water is penetrating, how long that takes and how long it stays moist at 12–18 inches deep.

You can dig down with your hands to check moisture, but I recommend buying a soil probe. These devices poke deep into the soil, and when you pull it out it extracts a soil sample with all of the soil layers intact. This enables you to easily check the soil conditions without making a mess.

TRELLISING AND TRAINING

It is difficult to explain to someone who has never grown cannabis how important it is to physically support your plants. I think this visual will help: each branch is in actuality like a grape vine. Each branch will grow a cluster of flowers towards the tip, which weigh about the same as a bunch of grapes. Those flowers grow heavier if they are rained on. Branches, like grapevines, cannot independently support the weight of these flowers and need to be held up. Without proper support, the branches can snap and die. With all of the work you are putting into this project, I guarantee that you will not want to watch big, beautiful branches covered in big, frosty flowers snap off and die before they are ready to harvest—this will break your heart.

Not only do branches need support to hold the weight of flowers, they also need support to protect them from wind and other random elements that can move your plants around. When your plants are small, around a foot or so, their stalks are still fairly malleable. They bend and sway when jostled or pushed around with light winds. However, there is a limit to how much force they can handle.

One year, I remember taking a walk to the river near my farm. It was so windy near the water that I quickly returned home.

The wind was blowing strong at home too, but I did not think too much of it. The next day I walked around my garden and discovered that a row of plants that I had neglected to sufficiently trellis had toppled over. I could hardly believe my eyes. Sadly, no matter how much I tried, I was never able to fully erect these plants again. That was a bummer. I learned a great lesson that day: sufficient plant support is a critical dimension of cultivating. Just like the children in your life, it is essential to provide your plants with support and structure in order for them to thrive.

Staking

In the early stage of a plant's life, supporting it is easy. You will need two materials: a ⅛-inch bamboo pole and a small zip tie. Once a plant is about a foot tall, stick the pole into the plant's pot, all the way in until the stick hits the bottom of the pot. I like to stick the pole in right next to the base of the stalk. Next, use the zip tie to loosely connect the plant and the pole. Connecting at the 6-inch point or above is preferable. I emphasize a loose connection because you want the plant to have space to grow through the zip tie. You do not want the plant to feel constrained, just gently supported when or if it receives a push by a strong force. This stick will stay with the plant until the plant is transplanted into the garden. You will cut the zip tie and remove the stick only when an alternative support system is in place. I cannot emphasize enough that this is not an extra step—this support is a small yet essential safety measure.

Trellising

Once all of your plants are planted out into your garden, it is time to put in place a support system that will support your plants throughout the rest of the season. There are two different methods of trellising, which you will select depending on how you have designed your garden. If you are growing in rows, such as in a raised bed or if you have lined your pots up into rows, I suggest using a plastic netting called Hortanova trellising. You can find this trellising on the internet if your local garden center does not carry it. If you are growing in pots that you want to keep as individual stand-alone units, you can use extra-large tomato cages or make your own plant cages with hog wire fencing.

Hortonova trellising is rectangular and needs to be secured to T-posts, which are tall steel stakes on all four corners of each plant. I attach trellising to 12 to 14-foot T-posts with plastic zip ties. Make sure that trellising is laid very tightly over the plants, like a bedsheet, with zero slack. The trellising will stretch over time. You want about 12 to 18 inches between layers. Put layers on before they are needed. Plan on putting on at least 4 layers but possibly more.

Trellising is a complete lifesaver in the face of wind and rain, as it only takes one big gust of wind or one rain storm to topple plants that are not properly supported. The key to proper support is having a sufficient amount of trellising tied to a sufficient amount of T-posts. Large branches cannot and will not hold themselves up in windy or rainy conditions and should be completely supported by trellising. Branches will crack and break off of the stalk and will probably die, which can also lead to fungal infections inside the place of the break. Sometimes it is possible to save a branch by making a splint for it, but in my experience the success rate of splints is fairly low.

A full-grown plant in ideal conditions does not have any freedom; it is completely confined by tight layers of trellising. All branches will be supported by netting and thus cannot move freely in the presence of weather.

Finally, make sure to put up vertical walls of netting along the sides of the beds/rows/pots (as opposed to the layers which are laid horizontally). Make sure to put side walls on after you have put on 4 layers of horizontal layers. Once you put on side walls it will make it very difficult to put on additional layers of horizontal walls.

Once the first layer of trellising is on, make sure to remove the zip tie and bamboo stick. If the zip tie remains on the plant, it can strangle the stalk as it grows.

Ideally each plant will have a layer of trellising every 12–18 inches. The height of your T-posts and the size of your plants will determine how many layers of trellising you can put on. I have seen growers extend their T-posts by zip tying 1-inch bamboo poles to the top of each T-post. I strongly suggest that you use this method on plants that have overgrown their trellising by 18 inches or more. Once you have put on the final layer of trellising, you can put on vertical trellis walls along the sides of the beds, tightly and securely attached to the T-posts. In some cases, you might need to apply a second layer of walls if branches have well outgrown the first wall. If this happens, congratulations! Your plants must be enormous!

In my friend's Oakland garden, where we are growing in pots, we are using cages. The pots and plants are small enough to use large "Texas" tomato cages. These cages are larger than typical tomato cages and fold flat for easy storage. An alternative to large tomato cages is making your own cage out of hog wire fencing. You can customize the size of your cage to the size of your pot. An additional alternative, especially for plants in pots larger than 50 gallons, is using the Hortonova trellis, but instead of laying it over a row, simply cut pieces into squares and use them for individual plants. This will require encircling each plant with four T-posts (or an alternative form of large and sturdy posts) and then following the same methods provided above for using Hortonova trellising.

Training

When I was farming, I developed a habit of constantly grabbing branches and slipping them through holes in the netting that were farther and farther away from the trunk. This process of spreading the growth horizontally is called training. It felt like a fun game. Over time, my plants grew into fat bushes. Not only did this feel like a feminist statement, this process also maximizes the plants' overall exposure to light. It produces more "tops," or large floral clusters, and it makes the plants easier to harvest because they are shorter. I strongly encourage making a habit of monitoring plant growth and training branches every day in your garden.

I do need to mention that occasionally branches snap while you are trying to train them. The best way to prevent this problem is training branches when they are still young and supple. You can easily stretch and bend new growth, but established growth becomes rigid and will snap if too much force is applied. If you feel like you missed the training of a branch and it feels rigid, try slowly adjusting it over the course of a few days instead of trying to force it with a swift application of pressure. Older, more rigid branches require a slower, more gentle approach.

If you are using cages, either Texas tomato cages or those that you have made out of hog wire fencing, you will simply encircle the plant with the cage. You will gently pull branches through the holes in the cage. The cage will support the main stalk and branches that can rest on the cage. However, cages are comparatively terrible at keeping plants safe in the face of strong winds and rain. For this reason, I strongly recommend using Hortonova trellising if at all possible.

Thinning

Thinning is an art. When thinning, you will remove all excess growth so that air can adequately circulate and the plant can focus its energy.

Well fertilized plants will produce lots and lots of branches. By the time that plants go into flower, you want to end up with major branches that get lots of sun exposure. There are lots of spindly shoots, or small branches, that come off of the main stalk and larger branches that will never produce much flower, and these shoots need to be removed.

Thinning will happen twice: once in mid- to late June, well before flowering, and again in early to mid-August, once flowering has begun. In the first thinning you will decide what are going to be the major branches on each plant and thin out excess growth. You will do this again in August. In both cases, you are "clearing out" the interior of the plant of all excess shoots which will only produce spindly flowers. You want the energy of the plant focused into large, strong branches which will yield large flower clusters.

Part Three

PROTECTING YOUR PLANTS

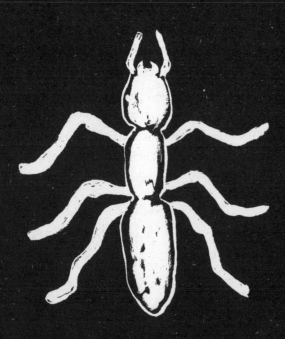

An ounce of prevention is worth a pound of cure. This saying is certainly true for cannabis cultivators. Thinking ahead and creating a pest/mold/theft prevention plan will save you time, money, heartache, and the use of lots of pesticides down the road. In this section I will discuss a wide range of practices that will prevent disaster from prevailing in your garden.

That said, bad things will happen to your garden. You will get mold. You will get pests. Your leaves will do weird things which the internet will diagnose as a dozen different nutrient deficiencies. Wind and rain will show up and destroy things. Timer batteries will die and fertigators will malfunction. You might even lose your entire garden because you forgot to turn your irrigation on or a deer found their way into your backyard. This project, like every project you have ever engaged in, will have problems. Become very comfortable with this fact. However, how you choose to approach these problems is up to you. I suggest that you prepare for these problems as best you can and also treat yourself and your garden with compassion when the problems hit, as I guarantee they will. This is life, after all.

PESTS

I believe that how people approach pest management usually tells you a lot about their personality. Here is my story:

When I first discovered that I had russet mites in my garden a few years ago, I immediately threw up my hands in surrender. I lost all sense of control and just let them take what I had worked so hard to cultivate. I passively accepted their presence and let them wreak havoc in my garden. Plant after plant bit the dust.

However, anger grew inside of me, and I eventually decided that I would not let these pests rob me of my garden. I leapt to the opposite end of the emotional spectrum and now wanted to wage an all-out war with these pests. I wanted a violent slaughter. I ordered carcinogenic pesticides and a hazmat suit. I was ready to destroy.

But once it was time to use these pesticides, I started to feel like this approach was way over the top. Sure, this would kill the pests, but it would also leave my garden and myself covered in poison, and it would decimate my integrity. Finally, I settled on a middle way. I would find a way to reclaim some of my garden with organic pesticides. I would spray vigilantly and assert my boundaries with these pests, but in a way that was safe for me and for the earth.

My approach to pest management is using organic pesticides to claim my power in my garden. It is fine if mites, aphids, and other "pests" live in the grass or the hillsides around my plants because I do not hate them, but it is not OK for them to live on and destroy the plants in my garden. It is my job to protect and defend each plant from pest damage, and this requires vigilance and assertiveness. Passiveness will not do the job, and synthetic/carcinogenic pesticides are harmful and completely unnecessary. Pest management is a way of asserting my boundaries in a way that is respectful to myself and the earth.

Integrated Pest Management

At my farm I use a well thought-out, Integrated Pest Management (IPM) plan that focuses on preventing and/or limiting pest outbreaks. IPM is a form of harm reduction rather than 100% prevention or eradication. This method of controlling pests uses a diverse array of tactics. Ultimately the aim is to reduce the cost of pest management, reduce the impact of pest damage, and reduce the exposure of people and the earth to synthetic pesticides. The IPM system at my farm includes:

- Active monitoring with weekly health walks

- Planting of multiple strains
- Working with pest resistant seeds and strains
- Use of diatomaceous earth for slug damage prevention
- Maintaining a properly ventilated and low humidity greenhouse
- Practicing careful watering practices, avoiding under- and overwatering
- Feeding plants adequately with fertilizer appropriate to the stage of growth
- Spraying with organic pesticides once pests have been discovered
- Infected leaves, branches and/or plants are physically removed from the garden
- Weak and/or pest infected starts are destroyed. Only the healthiest and most vigorous plants are planted out
- Thoroughly securing plants with trellising, especially low-hanging branches, to prevent damage by birds, dogs and/or cats
- In gardens where gophers are a known problem, plants are planted in pots or beds lined with gopher wire

Active Monitoring

There is a saying that the best fertilizer is a farmer's footsteps. The more time a farmer spends in the fields paying attention to the needs of their plants, the better their crops will do. This absolutely applies when it comes to pest management. Active observation is the first requirement of a strong IPM plan. I suggest taking a weekly "health walk" where careful attention is paid to the presence of pests and the nutrient and soil conditions of each plant, paying close attention to the "skirt," or the lower leaves, which are often the first to show signs of pest damage and nutrient deficiencies. My first year of farming I failed to do this and figured that since everything was on an automated drip system which was connected to a fertigator, all of my plants were fine. It was only after a few of my plants hovered near death that I noticed that their drip systems had long been clogged and the plants had not received water in I don't know how long. It is critical to pay careful, regular attention to the fine details of each plant.

As you actively monitor for pests, also keep your eyes open for herms. They happen, even to the best of us. Check every node of every plant if possible. Male flowers can appear anywhere throughout the season but are most troublesome during flowering. If you discover a plant that has hermed, destroy the whole plant. You do not want to risk that plant putting out more male flowers and pollinating all of your female plants. The risk is not worth saving the flowers from that one plant.

Using Pesticides

When I started growing weed, I was as Gaia-loving as they come. I am vegan, I eat organic veggies, I compost, I ride my bike, and I recycle. I love animals too! I never thought that I would ever use pesticides on plant medicine that I was growing with love. However, once I started investing lots of time and money into my garden, my tune changed. I did not want to lose everything I had to pests! I lost sleep over the decision of whether or not to spray my plants and I finally decided that I was comfortable spraying my plants with organic pesticides. Neem seed oil and essential oil sprays work really well for some fungal problems and mites. There are bacteria and soaps that you can spray that also work well. You can make your own pesticides and fungicides with household items like milk and/or hot peppers. This is one of those specialty areas that I suggest getting into during your second or third year. For your first year, I want the process to be as simple and successful as possible. For me, this means buying an organic store-bought pesticide and closely following the instructions indicated on the label.

Pests and Diseases Across the Seasons

Slugs, snails, aphids, and fungus gnats are the most common pests in the spring. These pests thrive in moist conditions. White flies, ants, and spider mites are other common greenhouse pests that need to be detected early and dealt with immediately. Fungal infections are also a critical challenge in the spring. Late spring and early summer are generally low-key when it comes to pests. This is because plants are growing rapidly and pest populations are just starting to get a foothold. This is a critical moment for pest detection and eradication. If you find any pests, immediately remove infected leaves and/or branches. Follow up physical removal with the use of pesticides on the infected plant. You can prevent an outbreak if you detect problems early and respond to them promptly and aggressively.

In late July, when plants are actively moving into the flowering stage, it is important that your plants are very well cared for and experience as little stress as possible. Stress suppresses your plants' immune systems, thus making it easier for pests to take hold. Make sure that plants are consistently well watered and are receiving enough nutrients to keep their leaves bright green. Continue to closely monitor for the presence of pests.

In August, prepare to spend some time spraying. I have never worked on a farm that did not have to spray for pests come August. Thrips, spider mites, russet mites, powdery mildew, and caterpillars are on the short list of potential pests. When spraying pests, make sure to keep a log of how much and how often you are spraying. Make sure that when you apply pesticides you are thoroughly spraying the undersides of leaves, the stalk of the plant, and the top layer of soil. These are all places where pests live.

Pests happen, and I believe that it is helpful to anticipate their arrival and plan accordingly rather than to flagellate yourself for not preventing them from showing up. If you have been closely monitoring your plants and have taken good care of them up until this point, you have certainly prevented lots of pests but most likely not all of them. Pests are very difficult to control; however, their presence and harm can be reduced.

In the year that I had russet mites I lost approximately 75% of my harvest to pest and mold damage. I was a new farmer, and bad stuff happens. In my second year, when I employed my well researched integrated pest management plan, my loss dropped to roughly 15–20%. It has hovered around this rate every year since. Hallelujah! Losing 75% of my crop was horrible, and I hope to never relive an experience like that again. On the bright side, it is now very easy for me to express empathy towards folks who are experiencing hopelessness and despair. I have been through the darkness.

Starting in September you will need to start addressing moisture-related problems again, namely root rot, powdery mildew, and botrytis (gray mold). These are all different types of fungal infections. Botrytis is that mold that makes it through your container of strawberries with lightning speed. One day all of your berries are just about ripe and the next moment most of them are inedible because they are covered in mold. Darn. This same process often happens to cannabis. When flowers are ripening, it is important to harvest them just as they reach their peak ripeness or a tiny bit before in order to save them from being attacked by gray mold, especially in moist conditions. Rain and morning dew can add just enough moisture to your flowers to promote the development of mold. Just as in strawberries, it spreads throughout cannabis flowers extremely quickly. I suggest starting to spray with an organic fungicide a week before the first rain and continue to spray every 7–10 days until you are 2 weeks away from harvesting.

There are so many different kinds of pests and solutions to getting rid of them. I suggest using Ed Rosenthal's book *Marijuana Pest and Disease Control* (2012) to assist with properly identifying and treating pests. That said, there are a few common pests and fungal diseases I will describe here.

Spider Mites

These mites live on the underside of leaves. They chew on the leaves, resulting in tiny specks the size of freckles that you can see by looking closely at the leaves. If you see white specks and turn the leaf over, you should see tiny little white bugs. You can treat spider mites with an organic miticide made out of pyrethrum, neem, citric acid, or essential oil blends that are sold as miticides. Commercially available products include Pyganic, Dr. Zymes, Grandivo, Trilogy, and Biomite.

Budworms

These are caterpillars that like to eat weed. They are difficult to love. They crawl through ripening colas, munching through buds and leaving a trail of poop. Mold usually develops where the caterpillars have damaged flowers. They are really destructive, and their populations can explode right under your nose if you are not paying close attention. The best treatment, once you have an infestation, is to scour your garden for them and pick them off of your plants manually. Next, spray with a caterpillar killer like Bt (Bacillus thuringiensis), which will make any remaining caterpillars sick.

Powdery Mildew

If you notice a white powder spreading across the leaves of your plants, you have powdery mildew, a.k.a. PM. You can treat this with a neem or citric acid-based fungicide such as Nuke 'em, Dr. Zymes, or Trilogy. There are also two products that use beneficial bacteria to treat fungal diseases: Serenade and Actinovate.

Botrytis

Gray mold will quickly spread through ripe flowers. The best way to deal with botrytis is to prevent it. Harvest flowers before rains. If your garden is experiencing dew in the morning or evening and your flowers are getting moist, closely monitor for mold and harvest as soon as any appears. Cut out all mold. You can spray with a fungicide to prevent mold, but if you do choose to spray, do not use neem, as it can leave a residual taste. I recommend using a citric acid or essential oil-based fungicide instead. Stop spraying 2 weeks before harvest or as indicated in the application instructions.

Damping Off and Root Rot

Damping off and root rot are the same thing, and there is no reliable treatment, so I strongly recommend focusing on prevention practices. The technical name of the fungus is pythium. Pythium is common where soil is kept soggy and humidity is high. You generally know that you have a pythium infection if part or all of your plant suddenly dies. Leaves will yellow and part, or all of the plant will droop and look dead. It is common for seedlings infected with pythium to die immediately (this is known as damping off), whereas large plants with root rot often lose one limb at a time until the entire plant is gone. It is important to make sure that your soil is cycling between wet and lightly moist. Low humidity and air circulation are also critical components of fungal prevention. If damping off or root rot do appear, discard your plants. Do not try and save young plants with fungal infections, as it will be next to impossible to cure them over the course of the season. If you start to lose a plant that has flowers that are nearly ripe, harvest them and process them as you would ripe flowers.

A critical component of pythium prevention is making sure that your grow container or hole in the ground has ample drainage. I had a friend who dug holes in the ground where the soil was primarily composed mostly of clay. She refilled her holes with fluffy potting soil. Sadly, the clay held the water used to irrigate the potting soil and left the plant roots continuously wet. She ended up having terrible problems with root rot. If your soil remains sopping wet, you are dramatically increasingly the likelihood of getting root rot. Second, I recommend avoiding plastic pots and containers, especially once plants are past the seedling stage. Plastic pots both hold in water and also prevent sufficient oxygen flow through the soil to the roots. I strongly recommend growing either in fabric pots, fabric lined raised beds, or directly in the ground as part of your pythium prevention plan.

SAFETY

I find it funny that I am writing about safety in a gardening book, but I would be completely irresponsible if I did not mention it. Cannabis plants can be extremely valuable. At the time of writing this text, a pound of dried and cured sun-grown cannabis flowers can be sold at roughly $1,000 wholesale and way, way, way more at retail. One medium yielding, outdoor cannabis plant can yield a pound, and I have seen plants that have yielded eight or more pounds.

Not only are these plants valuable, they exude a telltale aroma when they are ripening. Their aroma increases the closer the plants get to harvest. It is as if the plants are signaling aromatically that they are ready to be picked.

There are a few precautions that I can recommend for backyard growers. The first, the most important, and the most difficult is to keep your growing a secret. While you might want to tell your best friend, she might tell her boyfriend, and he might tell his brother who is desperate and might decide to rob you. The fewer people you tell, the safer you are.

My second recommendation is to grow your plants so that they are completely out of sight of neighbors and people who pass by your garden. If people see your plants, your secret is out. Again, the more people who know about what you are doing, the higher the potential for theft.

Finally, once your flowers have been harvested and cured, store them in a dry, cool, dark, and safe place. If your home is vulnerable to theft, consider storing your flowers somewhere else that is safer than your own home. Ultimately, keeping your business private and your valuables stored in a safe place will do a lot to keep you safe and your mind at ease.

Secrecy is a huge bummer for cannabis growers; however, it is your best defense against theft. You pour love into your garden, your plants grow up to be beautiful and covered with frosty flowers. You learn a ton and have a great time. You want to tell everyone and their mom about what you are up to, but in order to stay safe you should not tell anyone. What?!?! It is not fair. It is hard. I get it. However, it is a great lesson in humility. You get to pat yourself on the back, but please do not look for other people to pat you on the back by telling them your business. Let them love you for who you are, not for how big your plants are.

Secrecy is incredibly difficult when you are growing and sharing your flowers, which I hope all of the readers of this book ultimately do. You do not need to tell your community that you grew the medicine that you are sharing with them. I suggest telling them that it is organic and grown with love, but any more than that just puts you at risk.

Cannabis growing typically requires a high risk tolerance, and so I suggest taking an internal inventory of your personal risk tolerance while planning your garden. If you have a low risk tolerance, I suggest growing one small plant in a very discreet place. If you have a high risk tolerance, it is most important for you to be considerate of the risk tolerance of the people around you and make plans accordingly. You might be stoked to grow fifty plants, but that might make your roommates freak out. Check in with them and get on the same page.

Finally, if growing makes you think about buying a gun or a bunch of guard dogs, please reconsider your decision to grow. My guess is that if you are considering protecting yourself with a firearm, this activity makes you feel scared, which makes sense. I wonder if the potential joy of this project is going to outweigh your experiences of anxiety and fear. Again, I suggest assessing your risk tolerance and only cultivating an amount and within conditions that you feel comfortable with.

Part Four

HARVESTING YOUR MEDICINE

Harvest is a sacred time for a cannabis grower. It is a time of year when the nights begin to cool and the leaves of trees begin to glow bright red, orange, and yellow before they drop to the earth. Summer gardens die back, and evening fog begins to snake through the mountain valleys and down city streets. Your cannabis plants will probably start to yellow as your flowers, or "colas," mature. Once your flowers are ripe they will reach a peak state, and then the plant will begin to die. Harvest is a time marked by both abundance and death. Perhaps most importantly for a grower, it is the magical time when all of the energy from the sun, water, moon, earth, your heart, and your veganic fertilizers are concentrated into the psychoactive crystals coating each flower. Once ripe, each cola is clipped from its mother plant and processed so that the unique integrity of each flower is perfectly preserved. If you properly harvest and cure your flowers, all of the cosmic energy that went into their formation will be held within each flower until you set them ablaze in a joint, a bong, or a pipe.

While living in Humboldt, I grew to love harvest because of how the work brought people together. In my town there were dozens of cannabis farms, and my guess is that there are thousands scattered throughout the rugged mountains of Humboldt. The neighboring counties also harbor thousands of small pot farms. Every harvest, each farm assembles a crew and organizes what has come to be known as the annual "trim scene." Every trim scene shares a few basic themes: the majority of workers are almost always women, the work consists of harvesting weed from the garden and trimming dry weed indoors, most crews live on the farm throughout the harvest season, and the work is paid relatively well. Some scenes are large, with twenty or more people, and some are tiny, with only two to three people hired to trim a few pounds. I have worked at nearly a dozen trim scenes, and what I love the most about them is the experience of sitting around a table with a group of weirdos, sharing stories, music, and podcasts. There is a cultural exchange that happens at these scenes among these counter-cultural women, and this exchange of knowledge and experiences is important. I am deeply saddened because I believe that trim scenes will soon be extinct. Trimmers are currently being replaced by trim machines, while the wages for trimmers fall every year.

As a backyard grower you probably will not need to organize a trim scene. However, as you cut down your plants and hang your flowers in your dry shed, take a moment to connect with the spirit of the thousands of women who have gone through these tasks year after year on small farms throughout California, Oregon, and Washington. Many of us experienced community and reveled in the experience of camping out for a few months while making a bundle of money to fund our art projects, graduate school tuitions, and trips to India and Bali. However, we all knew that we were risking our safety. I was fired from a job after I rejected the sexual advances of a farmer who came home drunk one night and let himself into my trailer. While this was not my only uncomfortable confrontation with sexism, I was very lucky compared to what many other women have experienced at trim scenes. As you pull in your harvest, connect with the women who have done this work before you; these are your ancestors, and we want to support you.

In order to create a clear picture of what to anticipate, I have broken down harvest into eight parts:

1. Prep
2. Wet harvest work
3. Drying

4. Dry harvest work
5. Trimming
6. Curing
7. Storing
8. Cleanup

Ultimately, the aim of all harvest activities is to take flowers at their peak stage of ripeness and preserve them in a way that maximizes their integrity. This requires that so many things go right. Your best bet for having things go right is starting off harvest fully prepared for what is to come.

PREP AND SUPPLIES

For harvest you will need to set up a dry room: a space for drying and curing your flowers. Ideally you can clear out space in your garage, basement, or a large closet. This space should be self-contained and solely designated for your harvest activities. In addition, your dry space needs to be cool, dark, clean, and safe. It will need a power source and somewhere to hang string or rope, which you will use to hang branches.

While these are the ideal conditions, I have seen people dry and cure their cannabis in many different kinds of places and spaces. The most important factors are that the space is dark, cool, clean and dry.

Dry room supplies:
- Parachute cord or equally strong rope or string
- Screws and a screwdriver
- Power strip
- Dehumidifier
- Hygrometer (unless your dehumidifier has one built in)

- Oscillating fan
- Heater

Once you have cleared out your dry space you will need to gather your harvest supplies. You will need a pair of clippers for wet harvesting and a pair of scissors for clipping off wet leaves. I recommend using garden gloves while harvesting to keep the resin off of your hands. The thinner the gloves, the better. You can use latex gloves instead, but I recommend staying away from disposable supplies as much as possible. You will need a clean tote or two for transporting harvested flowers into your dry room and a Sharpie marker and twisty ties for identifying strains as you hang them in your dry room.

For curing, you will need clean paper bags and white sticky labels. Most grocery stores will sell you a stack. For trimming, you will need sharp "trimming scissors," which are also known as hand pruners or pruning snips. You will also need CitriSolv, a citric acid-based cleanser, and a baking tray (or, if you want to collect your kief, use a Trim Bin). All of these products are available for sale online or at your local grow store.

For post-trimming work, you will need several turkey bags (goose size) or canning jars and several storage totes. You can use the same totes that you used to move around harvested flowers. Finally, you will need a scale, a notebook, and a pencil for all record keeping. This step is optional but is helpful for comparing yields between strains and comparing yields over the course of several years.

Harvest supplies:
- Dehumidifier
- Fan
- Small heater
- 1 pair of garden clippers

- 1 pair of large sewing scissors
- 1 pair of thin garden gloves
- 1 small tarp
- 1 camping chair
- 1 Sharpie
- 6–12 twist ties
- 6–12 (short) paper grocery bags
- 1 pack of sticky white labels
- 1 16-oz bottle of CitriSolv
- 1 baking tray or Trim Bin
- Turkey bags and/or canning jars
- 2 pairs of trimming scissors
- 2–3 clean plastic totes
- 1 kitchen scale (optional)
- 1 large pot or bowl (optional)
- 1 large sifter (optional)
- 1 notebook (optional)
- 1 pencil (optional)

WET HARVEST

Wet harvest refers to the process of clipping off flowers, their leaves and hanging them in the dry shed. When the plant still has moisture in it, you are still in the phase of wet harvest. Once the flowers are dry, you begin the second phase of harvest, which I call dry harvest. This phase includes taking the flowers down from their rack, curing them in paper bags, clipping the flowers off of their stalks, and trimming excess leaves off of each flower. Ultimately, the wet and dry phases together make up the general harvest period, which lasts roughly from late September to late November.

I use the method of successive harvesting. This means that you harvest colas as they ripen rather than harvesting an entire plant at once. When using the method of successive harvest, each plant will be harvested several times until only the tiniest flowers are left and those can all be harvested all at once. This process can last from several weeks to several months.

Starting in mid-September, you will look for colas that are ready to harvest. Usually all of the top colas on a plant will be done first. There are several indicators that a cola is ripe enough to pick:

1) **The top cola is rock hard like a big, fully-erect flower**
2) **At least 50% of stigmas have died back and have turned brown**
3) **The trichomes are turning amber**

In my experience, the firmness of the cola is the most important and easiest indicator to identify but look for all three. Some strains might not become rock hard, but their stigmas will die back and the resin will change color. Pay attention to your plants and use your best judgment about when to harvest using these criteria.

Harvesting flowers at the peak of their ripeness will result in you harvesting and preserving your flowers at their most potent, fragrant, and flavorful stage. Harvesting prematurely will result in flowers with diminished quality and harvesting too late can result in loss of flowers to mold.

Harvesting at the correct time makes a huge difference in the ultimate quality of your dried flowers.

One year I hired someone to help me with the harvest at my farm. He was overeager and harvested many plants well before they had achieved peak ripeness in an attempt to save these plants from developing mold. Ultimately, the quality of the flowers was far inferior to plants grown from the same seeds a year earlier, but which were harvested at peak ripeness. It was a sad lesson and hopefully one that you will not repeat.

On the other hand, one year I waited until my Sour Diesel had reached its ultimate peak of ripeness, and then it rained. It took me a few days to harvest everything, I had quite a few plants and ended up filling several wheelbarrows full of moldy colas. They had been so close to perfection and then they were destroyed so quickly. Do not let this be you. If rain is coming, harvest a little early.

Once you have found colas that are ready to harvest, wait until a cool part of the day or night and start clipping ripe colas. I suggest harvesting colas in uniform lengths with clean, sharp clippers. Harvest branches in sections that are between 10 and 12 inches long. You want to harvest sections that are consistently the same length.

It is important to wait until a cool time so that the trichomes are cool, which makes them less sticky. When flowers are warm, the resin coating them becomes very tacky and will cover everything it touches. When colas are harvested while they are still warm from the sun, dirt, leaves, dust, etc. will stick to them as they move through the harvest process. Harvesting colas when they are cool makes the process a whole lot less messy.

Next, you will fill totes with ripe colas. You can pile them gently into the totes, but never, ever try and apply pressure on them to squeeze in more colas. This will cause the large leaves, or "fan" leaves, to stick to the colas and will make it difficult to clip them off later. This can also damage the trichomes, which you want to be very gentle with. When looking for ripe colas, make sure to thoroughly check the tops of plants, where colas are hard to see but typically finish first.

When harvesting, make sure to keep like strains together. I recommend harvesting one strain at a time. This way you can harvest your strain, process it, hang it in the dry shed, and label it. Repeat for the next strain. This will keep strains from mixing and causing confusion later on.

Harvest Problems

There are three major issues of concern that often arise while harvesting. The first issue is surprise strains. Whether you have grown from seed or clone, you might end up with a plant that is not what you thought it was going to be, and sometimes you will not notice until you are harvesting. If you are growing several plants of the same strain, you can harvest them together; however, if you notice that one of the plants is different from the rest, stop harvesting that plant with the others and tag it. Defining differences include flowers smelling different and/or having leaves that are shaped differently or are a different color. Once you have identified that the plant is different from the rest, give it a new name that indicates that it is different from the others and harvest it as a separate strain. Not only is this surprise common, it is almost to be expected considering the lack of regulations of clone and seed sales. Perhaps this problem will end once the industry becomes more regulated, but until that time, keep a close eye out for plants that seem different from the others of the same strain.

The phenotypic qualities of your flowers will not change during the drying and curing process. Therefore, do not expect that plants labeled as the same strain will become more alike during the harvest process. They will not. One year I grew out a dozen or so Blue Dream plants. We were halfway into harvesting them when it was brought to my attention that two of the plants smelled different than the rest. I took a look at them and not only did they smell different, their leaves were a lime green, whereas the rest of the plants had leaves that were a deep forest green. I realized that these "stray" plants smelled skunky like a Kush rather than sweet like Blue Dream. Unfortunately, the flowers from these plants were now well mixed into the already harvested "true" Blue Dream flowers. I was frustrated but learned my lesson to carefully check plant phenotypes before harvesting to make sure that all of the plants that are marked as the same strain do, in fact, share the same characteristics.

The second issue that will arise is mold and pest damage. One year I was helping someone harvest and as we clipped ripe colas, we started to realize that the plants were covered in budworms, which burrow into the bud and are difficult to see by quickly glancing at colas. Most of the colas had some budworm damage. Once this realization was upon us, we began to clip as many colas as we could before they were damaged by more worms and before the damage turned to mold, which would spread rapidly through the colas, making them completely unsalvageable. Our harvest plan had to be completely adapted to the new realities of pest damage. We worked urgently and harvested colas that were on the verge of ripeness, which, in pest-free circumstances, we would have left to ripen for a few more days.

In another circumstance, I was harvesting on my own farm and discovered powdery mildew on the underside of the canopy of several Super Silver Haze plants. This led to an increased pressure to remove as many of the flowers as I could from the garden to save them before they were covered in powdery mildew.

Ultimately, pest presence and pressure will cause adjustments to your harvest plan. You might have to decide whether to harvest plants that are not quite ripe or leave them to ripen with the risk of incurring pest and mold damage. This is a tough decision that farmers and gardeners of all stripes come upon at one time or another.

One great tip I always use during harvest is to keep an eye out for a single brown or yellow leaf sticking out of a cola. If you happen to notice a dead leaf coming out of an otherwise alive cola, it is most likely an indicator of mold inside of the cola at the base of the leaf. My guess is that the leaf dies for some reason and, as it decomposes, mold grows on and around the leaf. In any case, if you see one of these telltale leaves, open up the cola and check for mold. You will probably want to harvest the entire cola, but if it is far from being ripe, you can clip away the flowers around the dead leaf area. If the brown leaf goes ignored, it is highly probable that mold will spread throughout the cola and you will lose the entire cola. This random leaf can also be a sign of caterpillar presence, so make sure to check the cola for any signs of their munching or poop.

The final issue is related but slightly different. If you have plants that are approaching ripeness and you know that rain is in the forecast, you will have to decide whether or not to harvest your plants slightly early or risk them getting wet, which will exponentially increase the likelihood that colas will develop gray mold, which will destroy the plants' flowers. This is a very difficult decision to make.

PROCESSING YOUR HARVEST

Hanging

Once flowers have been harvested and collected into a plastic tote, you will need to head to your dry, clean, well lit place to work. Spread out your small tarp and set out a second tote and your camping chair. Take a seat and pull both bins close to you. You will use your large scissors to clip off all fan leaves. The leaves will fall onto the tarp, unless you want to clip leaves over a tote and collect leaves there. This is not an exercise in detail; in fact, it is an exercise in efficiency. The reason that we deleaf is to fit more flowers into the dry shed. Removing leaves at this time is not necessary, but it is helpful if you are short on dry space. Gently place the deleafed colas into the second tote. These colas are ready to hang.

Colas should never, ever sit in totes for multiple hours, and harvested colas need to always stay out of the sun, heat, and rain. If you have an emergency and it is absolutely necessary for you to take a break after harvesting and you cannot immediately clip leaves and hang your colas, make sure to store your tote in a cold, dry, dark place, like a shed or basement.

While deleafing, make sure to open up big colas to check for mold hiding inside of them. This should be a quick check, but it is an essential part of the process. If you see any gray mold or powdery mildew while deleafing, clip it out. Absolutely all of it. Moldy flowers can be composted along with the leaves.

In your dry shed you will need to hang lines across the ceiling where you will hang your colas. If you have grown a pound or more of flowers, you may consider using a method that I developed. It originated as the "Humboldt Hang," but I have created a few modifications which I really like. It will require several additional materials.

Hanging dry rack materials:
- Plastic mesh fencing with 2" holes (optional)
- Small carabiners
- Strong rope

Below I will explain how to hang-dry using either a hanging rack or single string. If you have grown more than one tote full of wet flowers, I suggest using a rack. With anything less, I would use a single string to hang all colas.

For your drying rack, you will need to string a piece of rope tightly across the ceiling of your dry space. Use your screws and screwdriver to create places where you can attach your rope. Attach your rope to the screws and pull it as taut as possible. Roll out your mesh fencing (also known as landscape fencing, garden netting, etc.) and cut a piece that stretches from the rope to a foot above the floor. Use the carabiners to secure the fencing to the rope. Use as many carabiners as it takes to ensure that the fencing hangs flat and does not develop "waves." If you cannot find small carabiners, you can use zip ties. I prefer carabiners because they are reusable. The rope should be strong and taut enough that the weight of the fencing does not cause it to sag.

If you are hanging from single pieces of rope, you will hook colas onto the rope by wedging the rope between a flower and the stem. You can hang the colas fairly close together, especially if there is no mold present. If they touch and even overlap a little, that is fine as long as your weed is mold-free.

Hang all of the colas from one strain in a line and then use your twisty tie to label the strain. Label the twisty tie and twist it onto the rope. If you have a second strain, follow the same directions and follow it with another labeled twisty tie. It might be helpful to draw an arrow on the twisty tie to indicate which side of the twisty tie the label is referring to.

If you are using the hanging rack, you will start hanging colas in a row at the bottom of the rack. You are going to stick colas partially into the holes and let them go. The tip of the cola should fall down towards you, and the end of the cola will stick up on the opposite side of the fencing. It should carefully balance in place. Do not hook buds onto the mesh fencing, as this will make taking them out of their holes, once they are dry, very difficult and time consuming. When you hang (balance) your first few colas, make sure that they clear the floor by at least 6 inches. If they do not, remove them and hang them higher on the rack until there is at least 6 inches of clearance.

You will determine where to hang your second line by sticking a cola through at a point where the tip of the flower hangs right above where the cola below sticks through the netting and hangs down. Hang your second line of colas across the rack. Continue this process until the entire hanging rack has been covered with colas, or until you run out of colas to hang. Hanging in rows with colas of a consistent length, making sure not to hook or ensnare them on the rack, makes the process of taking your flowers down a total breeze. You will be able to take down row after row, slipping colas out of the holes in the rack where they are resting without much hassle, if any at all.

Once you are done hanging, label a twisty tie and twist it onto the hanging rack where the flowers are hanging. If you have only covered part of the rack, make sure to leave a large and very noticeable gap between the strain that you have just hung and the next strain that you will hang above this strain. Make sure that it is visually unmistakable that there are two (or more) different sections hanging on the rack. Label each section appropriately.

If you have individual buds, which are smaller flowers and usually the size of nuggets, you can hook them onto the rope or mesh fencing. If you have a lot of these, consider buying a circular hanging rack, otherwise known as an herb drying rack. Make certain that you include identifying tags in every single section. You can fill the circular drying rack to be very full, as the flowers shrink quickly. If any branches or buds fall, pick them up immediately. If something is left on the ground, the likelihood of it getting stepped on, dirty, wet, or forgotten about is extremely high. Just deal with it immediately.

In your dry room, you will need a fan, a dehumidifier, and a heater. If your dehumidifier does not have an internal humidity monitor, you will need to buy one; it is called a hygrometer. You will need to use a combination of this equipment to keep your dry room between 45–55% humidity and between 65–75 degrees. Keeping your dry room within this range is essential for the proper drying of your flowers. Low temps and high humidity will extend the amount of time it will take to dry out flowers, and this can lead to the growth of mold and mildew.

Drying

Properly drying, or "curing," your flowers is an extremely important process and can make or break the quality of your flowers. Drying should take 5–12 days. Drying too quickly can result in a "green" or "harsh" taste, and drying for an extended period can increase the likelihood that gray mold or mildew will grow in your flowers.

Monitoring the dry space starts with regularly checking the humidity level and the room temperature. It is critical to keep humidity levels stable at 45–55% and room temperature between 65–75 degrees. If the humidity rises above 55%, you might need a higher powered dehumidifier. If it is cooler than 65 degrees, you need to warm up the room. If it is too warm, turn on the fan and open a window or a door.

My first year working in Humboldt was extremely rainy. One weekend my boss had to leave town and left a taco truck (yes, a former food truck) filled with hanging racks of cannabis to dry. Unfortunately, the humidity was too high for too long in the truck, and mold spread rapidly from rack to rack. When he returned from his trip, he discovered that the majority of the cannabis in the truck had molded and needed to be destroyed. It was a pitiful scene. Do not let his mistake be your mistake! Make sure to regularly check your humidity levels, especially if you are trying to dry in a taco truck in the middle of a storm. In fact, it is helpful to have a dry room that is tightly sealed, where all windows are covered.

Finally, keep the dry space clean. Remove totes that are not in use. Sweep up if there is an accumulation of debris on the floor. There should be no trash or clothing left in the dry space. This is a special space. You will also need to regularly check to make sure that the power is on, that the dehumidifier is working properly, and, if your dehumidifier is connected to a hose that automatically drains out water, make sure that there are no kinks in the hose that would prevent proper drainage. If your dehumidifier has a water catchment system, make sure to dump the water regularly.

Pay attention to what is going on during harvest in the same way that you paid attention to your seedlings and to the development of pest problems. This is not a time for you to check out. In fact, your attention is most necessary in this final hour. All of your hard work could end up in the compost if you do not pay close and careful attention to all of the details of harvest. Breathe deeply and remember that you got this.

Taking Down and Storing

Continue to monitor each strain until the sticks of a batch can slowly snap. This means that you slowly bend the stalk until it snaps. If the stalk folds instead of snaps, then it needs more drying time. It is critical to wait until this point. Do not, under any conditions, take flowers down until after the stalk can do a slow snap. Wait until all of the flowers of a batch are dry until you start to take any down. Just wait.

Once the stalks of a batch are all slow snapping, it is time to remove the dried flowers from the dry room. When taking down your flowers, the first step is to check the twisty tie of the area that you are preparing to take down. Make sure that you are clear where the section for this twisty tie begins and ends.

When taking down dry colas, gently remove them from the fencing. Put them into paper bags with stems down and flowers pointing up. This will keep the tip of the cola from being smashed. Fill paper bags until they are completely full. Make sure to label each bag. Write the strain names on sticky white labels and stick these onto the bags. These bags do not need to be sealed. The labels make it easier to see the strain name, and if you reuse the bags, you can simply cover up the first label with a second. You are using paper bags because they draw any remaining moisture out of the flowers. Also, paper is a breathable material that will enable moisture to escape rather than trapping it inside of the bags and the flowers. Make sure that every single paper bag is labeled before it leaves the dry space.

Once you have taken down a batch, make sure to remove the twisty tie that indicated that strain. Make sure to only take down the flowers from the section that you are working on. It is easy to become overzealous and to start pulling down flowers from neighboring sections, so again, make sure that you are paying attention.

Check the ground to make sure that flowers have not fallen onto the ground. If you find any, grab them and throw them into an appropriate bag, but only if they were on the ground for less than five seconds. Haha.

Once bags are filled and labeled, they can either stay in the dry room or be moved to an equally dry and dark place for the final stage of curing. Flowers will remain in paper for several days, until they are at a moisture level that you feel comfortable with. This step stabilizes their moisture. It is a security step. You do not want your flowers so dry that they start to crumble apart, but in my experience, flowers only reach this stage when they are near wood stoves, which are both dry and hot. In Humboldt County, where many people live off the grid, wood stoves are often used instead of dehumidifiers. That said, you can always remoisten flowers later. So, too dry is better than not dry enough.

Once the flowers are at a moisture level that you are happy with, you can transfer them into turkey bags (the large goose size). Flowers can remain in turkey bags until it is time to trim them. If they are going to stay in turkey bags for a prolonged period, make sure to open up and "burp" your bags periodically to allow any trapped moisture to escape.

For prolonged storage, you can keep your bags of flowers in totes and store those in a dry, dark, cool place. A popular alternative in Humboldt is storing bags of flowers in large pickle barrels. These are cheap, have a seal that keeps them watertight, and are very large; however, they usually still smell like pickles or pepperoncinis. They might even come with a few free pepperoncinis still inside. This has happened to me. In my experience, this smell does not transfer to the flowers, but it does stick to the bags. Needless to say, if you use a pickle barrel, make sure to thoroughly clean and dry it out first. Many growers bury their pickle barrels in the ground to keep their flowers cool, since the ground stays cool throughout the year. For most backyard growers, this is not an option; however, if you can store your barrel in a basement or an equally cool place, this is ideal. It is very helpful to clearly label each tote or barrel with the strain of flowers inside.

Trimming

Trimming is the process of clipping all of the excess leaf off of your flowers. The excess leaf will not have very many trichomes on it compared to the flower. By trimming off the excess leaf, you will be left with buds that are coated in trichomes, which are the crystals that are rich with psychoactive THC. In addition, a well trimmed flower, or "nug," is clipped in such a way that it has the minimum amount of stem. Just like the leaf, the stem is not covered in trichomes, and so clipping it out ensures that you are left with as little excess plant material as possible. Trimming happens after your flowers have been cured and before they are put into winter/spring storage.

Before you begin trimming, you will need to assess the moisture levels of your flowers. If the flowers you are working with are so dry that they start to crumble apart, you can rehydrate them by putting ½ of a conventional corn tortilla into the turkey bag with the flowers and sealing the bag. Let the tortilla sit in the bag for a few hours. The moisture from the tortilla will spread to the flowers. If the tortilla completely dries out and the flowers are still too dry to trim, add a second ½. (I know you want to use an organic tortilla, but do not do it. Organic tortillas grow mold easily and this mold can spread to the flowers. Conventional tortillas do not grow mold, which is weird but helpful.) If your flowers are too wet, put them into paper bags and place them in your dry room at 55% humidity and between 65–75 degrees. Leave the flowers in the room until they are sufficiently dry.

Once your flowers are at a desirable moisture level to trim, you can snip them off of their stalks into a large turkey bag.

I recommend filling a turkey bag with dried flowers and finding a workplace that is comfortable, cool, and clean. In order to reduce my mess, I start by laying down a tarp or sheet on the floor and sitting my camping chair on top of the tarp, just like when you were clipping off fan leaves. I like to trim sitting in a camping chair because they are cheap, easy to store, fairly comfortable, and they have a little cup holder where you can keep your cup of CitriSolv solution and your scissors. If you choose a different kind of chair, make sure that it is something you don't mind getting covered in resin, or cover it with a sheet before trimming in it.

I wear thin gloves and an apron while I trim. The gloves keep the resin off of my fingers. I like to use thin gardening gloves, which are reusable. Most trimmers I know use disposable latex gloves, but by the end of the season you end up throwing away a ton of plastic. Booooo. I wear an apron so that any trim that falls onto me falls onto the apron, which makes cleaning myself off much easier. It is nice to find an apron with a front pocket where you can store your phone or whatever knickknack you need on you at all times.

Here are my recommendations for trimming flowers so that they are conventionally beautiful. These standards are mostly based on the practice of taking away all of the excess plant material that does not have THC coating it and leaving the smoker with nugs that have minimal stem and maximum smokable flower. However, this practice has evolved into an art where trimmers transform shaggy nuggets into smooth and tight-looking spheres. The problem with this transformation process is that you end up trimming away lots of perfectly good flower coated in THC in order to smooth out your buds. Ultimately, you end up with less flower to smoke, but it looks professionally manicured.

In order to get the "professionally manicured" look, every flower should end up being between the size of a lighter and a dime. If the flower is larger, you can pull off parts of the flower until it is no larger than the size of a lighter. If a flower is smaller than a dime, you can set it aside and keep your "b-buds" together. Or you can trim them if you do not have problems with small flowers. In the professional world of cannabis buying and selling, there is a prejudice against smaller buds because they are looked at as if they are "crumbs" and thus worth less. Most farms where I have worked discard all of their small buds into trim bags because farmers know that buyers do not want to purchase these crumbs. As a home grower, I think it would be silly to toss your small buds in with your trim, but you need to make the decision that feels right for you.

I always tell trimmers to make the flower "naked" of all excess leaf. At this point, leaf that you are trimming away is primarily the part of the flower that makes the sides of the flower uneven and shaggy. You want to trim this away to create a flower, or "bud," that is smooth on all sides. You will do this by picking the leaf away with the tip of your trimming scissors rather than trying to shave the flowers with the entire blade of your scissors. Shaving your flowers will also shave off THC- and CBD-rich trichomes. Be gentle with your trichomes. Don't forget to snip off the "crows feet," which are the two leaf stems at the base of each flower.

Make sure to clip the stems as short as possible without causing the flower you are trimming to fall apart. Long, sharp stems can tear holes in bags and are commonly thought of as unsightly. Even if you are storing your flowers in glass, you might gift some to a friend who wants to store your flowers in a plastic bag, and those sharp stems will poke right through. Keep those stems short.

I like to set up my trim tray with three yogurt tubs lined up horizontally on the side of the tray closer to my knees while I leave the space closer to my stomach free. Next, I grab a handful of loose flowers from the turkey bag and drop them into the first tub on the left. As I work, I grab handfuls of flowers from this tub with my left hand and trim them one by one. This means that I am holding a few flowers in the palm of my hand while my thumb and pointer finger are holding a bud while I trim it. The trim falls onto the free space on the tray. If I end up with a b-bud, I drop it into the second yogurt container. Trimmed buds go into the third yogurt container. Next, I roll another flower out of my palm and between my thumb and pointer finger.

When my palm is empty of buds, I grab another handful of flowers. When my mound of trim has piled high on my tray, I scoop it up and dump it into a clean turkey bag that you will use specifically to collect your trim. Once you have a yogurt container full of trimmed flowers, pour them into a second clean turkey bag and tie the turkey bag shut. Do the same thing with your b-buds and pour them into a third turkey bag.

When my scissors get sticky, I dip them into a glass of CitriSolv mixed with water and clean this solution off with a rag. I like to have at least two pairs of scissors so that while I am working my second pair is soaking in the solution. When the pair that I am working with becomes too sticky, I put them into the CitriSolv solution and clean off the pair that were soaking. I strongly encourage you to keep your scissors clean while you work. The stickier your scissors are, the more difficult trimming will be. Make life easy for once by keeping your scissors gunk-free.

Clip out and compost all flowers with any signs of mold or mildew. I recommend trimming out the area closest to mold to ensure that the majority of mold spores are removed. You do not want to share moldy weed with your friends. This is not OK.

Always keep your flowers out of the sun, away from humidity and heat. Once I was trimming for a friend and made myself comfy on the front porch of the cabin where I was living. I was clueless and set the turkey bag with untrimmed flowers next to me in direct midday sunlight. As I trimmed, I noticed that the flowers were extremely dry; in fact, they were the driest, most crumbly flowers I had ever worked with. They simply fell apart as I worked with them. I remember thinking to myself, "This poor woman—she overdried her flowers. Now they are all falling apart. This really sucks." Half of the crumbly flowers ended up in the trim bag. It was only in retrospect, years later, I realized that I had been baking those poor flowers under the light and heat of the sun. Now I feel bad. Once again, do not let this be you.

Once you have filled a turkey bag with trimmed flowers, b-buds, or trim, knot the bag closed, label it with a white sticky label, and put it into the tote or pickle barrel where your flowers are being stored. You can also store your trimmed flower in glass jars if you feel uncomfortable storing your flowers for prolonged periods in plastic. I know you folks are out there and I love you.

Once you have filled up a turkey bag or a mason jar, label it and seal it shut. If there is any indication that the flowers have been remoistened, return them to the dry room and thoroughly dry them out before they are put away.

Finally, I want to remind you to be very careful about what goes into your turkey bags. One year I was trimming and eating snacks the entire time. When my boss went to weigh out what I had trimmed, he discovered a few chocolate chips in my bag. I thought it was funny. He did not. From his perspective, he could have lost $2000 of flowers due to my carelessness, if the chips had melted. So, just be careful with your flowers. Keep your cats away, keep your water bottle tightly closed, and make sure that you do not let your chocolate chips creep into your trim bag. Pay attention to what you are doing. The smallest of mistakes can have consequences that you never intended. If you want your flowers to be spectacular and free of crumbs and dog hair, then make sure to work in a clean space and pay attention to what you are doing. OK, moving on.

Finally, finally, I do need to remind you that this is your cannabis, and so you should trim it however you want to. In fact, if you want to leave it untrimmed, that is perfectly fine. Be different!

Trim

If you intend to make hash or butter with your trim, aka shake, sort out sticks, fan leaves, and mold as you go. Dispose of these in a compost pile or green bin if you have one. These items should not be included in your trim bag. I mix the trim from all of my strains, but some people like to keep the trim of each strain separate. This depends on whether or not you care about your hash being single strain or a mix of strains. This is really your call. Keep your trim bag closed and out of direct sunlight at all times. You want the trim to stay cool, dry, and fresh. Once your trim bag is full, seal it closed. Open the bag once a week for a month. At this time your trim will be stable and remain fresh as long as it is kept in a cool, dark, and dry place.

Finger hash

While you work, you will accumulate resin on your fingertips. This is finger hash! I recommend rolling it into little balls and storing these in an airtight jar in the refrigerator or freezer. You can smoke these with flowers or on their own with a hash pipe.

If you are using a trim bin, you will collect a white powder known as kief on the tray beneath your work screen. Kief is another form of hash. As with the finger hash, I recommend collecting it and storing it in an airtight jar in the fridge or somewhere cool and dark. Hash is organic plant material and can grow mold, which is why it is important to store it properly. I will explain how to make cold water hash in a later section.

Post-Trimming Work

Trimming is very time consuming and labor intensive. I like to use that time to listen to lots of podcasts and audiobooks. Maybe you are better at mindfulness than I am and you want to use this time to be in the moment. You go girl! Regardless of how you make your way to the end, trimming all of your weed is a wonderful accomplishment to be very proud of. However, there is still plenty of work to be done before your harvest is complete.

Once your flowers are trimmed, store them in plastic totes or pickle barrels. However, if you are curious about how much you yielded and are into keeping records, you can follow the instructions below.

For this step, you will need your notebook, a scale, a large kitchen pot or bowl, a large sifter, and a clean storage tote.

First, pour the flowers into the sifter and sift out all of the trim. Sift above the clean storage tote. Once sifted, collect the trim that fell into the tote and add it to your other bags of trim. Turn on the scale and set the bowl/pot onto the scale. Press the "on" button, which will set the scale to zero, and then set the scale to measure grams. Pour the sifted flowers into the pot/bowl. Record the date, strain, and number of grams in your notebook. Return the flowers to their original turkey bag and seal it closed with a knot. Return this bag to flower storage. Easy! Done! This is an exciting moment, and it deserves a little dance. I like to do the robot. However, harvest is still not over until everything has been cleaned up.

Finally, it is time to clean up! Use your CitriSolv solution and rags to clean bins, scissors, clippers, and everything else that is covered in resin. Remember, anything that has resin on it will continue to smell like weed indefinitely. Either clean it, throw it away, or wholeheartedly embrace the constant smell of cannabis.

Part of the cleanup process is chopping down your plants and removing the root ball. At this point, your plant is probably dead and beginning to rot. I like to clean out dead plants from my garden before winter because leaving them in place feels messy. However, if you want to leave your plants in the ground until the spring as a reminder of what once was, then go for it. If you want to remove your plants and you have a sawzall, this is a great tool for chopping down your plants, especially if they are really large. If your plants are smallish, you can try and pull them out of the soil and chop the plants up with clippers. If you have access to a chipper, I recommend chipping your plants and using the chips to mulch your garden or adding it to compost piles. If you do not have a chipper but you have a municipal compost bin, chop your plants into the smallest pieces possible and load them into your compost bin. All excess leaf and sticks from your plants can also be composted. At this point, you should have piles of leaf from wet harvesting and sticks left over after you bucked flowers off of branches. If you do not have a bin, chop all of your plant matter up into small bits and find a place to pile all of your plant matter and let it sit out in the weather and rain all winter. This should help it to break down, and in the spring, you can turn fold it into your soil.

You can leave your irrigation set up over the winter, but bring your fertigator and timer indoors. If you have netting that is reusable, roll it into small balls and label them with their dimensions or the location where they were used. Keep plant stakes and/or plant cages together in an out of the way place, ideally indoors.

Once you have stored your harvest and cleaned up, it is really time to celebrate! Roll one up, take your bra off, and kick back. I am really proud of you and hope that you feel a sense of accomplishment. You did it! Hurray!

Winter Monitoring

There is one final task left which you need to do in order to preserve this year's harvest. During the winter months, it is essential to regularly check the moisture level of flowers and adjust them if necessary. To check moisture levels, simply open up bags of flowers and feel the flowers. If they seem like they have remoistened at all, you will need to pour your flowers into paper bags and sit them next to a dehumidifier until they are bone dry. Then you can pour them back into their plastic bags and return them to storage. Opening plastic bags (or mason jars) will also allow any accumulated gases to escape. This is an important part of the curing process. It is important to check moisture levels every few weeks through the winter months. Eventually, your flowers will stabilize and you can keep them in storage until you need them.

HARVESTING ALL OF THE EXTRAS

One great thing about cannabis cultivation is that you end up yielding so much more than organic, sun-grown flowers. Fresh cannabis juice, wood chips, kindling, kief, and hash are a few of the additional gifts that the plants offer. In addition, you can easily make cannabis-infused tinctures, salves, and butter. Here are a few methods for harvesting or producing these products.

Fresh Cannabis Juice

In Humboldt County there is a well-known doctor who advocates for the juicing of fresh cannabis leaves. I will not extol the health benefits here because they are unsubstantiated; however, all of that chlorophyll has got to be good for you. The best time to use the leaves for juice is in the spring, when they are the most supple and are free of dust and pesticides. Clip the leaves off of the stalk and throw them into your blender or juicer. Easy. You can also freeze leaves for adding to smoothies later. If you are curious about learning more about cannabis leaf juice, you can research Dr. William Courtney on the internet.

One season I juiced a lot because I used regular seeds and there were lots of males to kill. One day I made a quart of juice and sipped on it all morning. I went to a friend's house for a meeting of our meditation group. As the meeting started, I realized that I was really high. I do not know how the juice could have had a psychoactive effect because my understanding is that in order for cannabis to make you high, the THC must be decarboxylated (heated above 220 degrees Fahrenheit), and this certainly was not. I suggest that you start with a little bit of cannabis leaf juice and gradually work your way up to drinking more, and monitor how it affects you.

Kief

Kief refers to the dry trichomes that fall off of dried buds, usually during the trimming process. Kief is easy to harvest if you can get your hands on a trim tray designed to collect it. In Humboldt the most popular brand of these trim trays is the "Trim Bin." This tray is composed of two separate trays that fit together. You trim into the top tray, and the bottom of it is lined with a mesh screen. The first tray sits snuggled inside of the second tray, which is made out of plastic and collects the kief that falls through the mesh screen. After trimming a batch, lift up the top tray and collect the kief by brushing it into a small pile with the brush that comes with the tray and scoop it into an airtight jar with a spoon. Do not rub flowers against the tray, as this will cause them to fall apart, and you will have pieces of flower in your kief, which will dilute the purity of the kief. I know purity sounds so old paradigm, but in this circumstance, it seems fairly harmless. You can use the kief by sprinkling it onto your flowers before you smoke them.

Wood Chips and Kindling

Once flowers have been harvested, you will be left with lots of little sticks. These make great kindling for fires, but they will send the smell of cannabis up and out of your chimney. If you have more than you can use for kindling, you can rent a chipper and chip the sticks and stalks. These chips are great for adding carbon to compost piles.

Infused Coconut Oil/Butter

For your infused coconut oil or butter, you will need 1 cup of coconut oil, 1 cup of trim, cheese cloth, a double boiler or slow cooker, and a glass jar or bowl with a lid. An alternative method is using cold water hash (no more than a cup) instead of trim, if you have some. Pour your oil and trim into your double boiler or slow cooker for 3–6 hours, stirring occasionally. Ideally your oil will heat up to 220–240 degrees; if it gets hotter, turn down the heat. Once the oil has simmered for a few hours, use the cheese cloth to strain out the trim or hash as you pour it into your glass bowl. Snap the lid closed and store your butter in the fridge or freezer. In order to find the right dose for you, start with an amount the size of ¼ tsp (if you used more than ¼ cup of hash, experiment in increments of ⅛ tsp) and wait 30 minutes. If this dose is not sufficient, eat another ¼ tsp. Continue with this experiment until you feel sufficiently dosed. Make sure to record how much oil it took to get to your ideal state of stoney-ness. This will help you to figure out how much to use in the future when you cook with it or spread it on toast.

Cooking with Cannabis

You can bake, sauté, and even add cannabis-infused oils to smoothies. Simply calculate how many servings you are planning to prepare and add the equivalent of that many doses to your food. For example, if I am making 12 cupcakes and my canna-coconut oil is 1 tsp/ dose, then I am going to replace 12 tsp of oil in the recipe with 12 tsp of my canna-coconut oil. The potency will not change as you cook with it. Make sure that your food is very well labeled and stored safely away from pets and children.

When I lived at a big hippie co-op in Berkeley, where I got my start as a gardener, people were accidentally dosed with cannabis and other psychedelics all the time because brownies, candies, and other edibles were left around the house without appropriate labeling. I had a roommate who was high for three days because she ate pizza that had been infused with cannabis oil without her knowledge. It was an awful experience for her. Preparing cannabis-infused foods without appropriate labeling and safe storage is completely irresponsible and has the potential to traumatize someone who is not feeling psychologically well and/or does not feel safe. Please be considerate and responsible when you cook and store your edibles.

Cannabis Salve

Lots of people like to use cannabis salve to cure muscle pain. It is fairly easy to prepare and makes a great gift. In a double boiler, mix 1 cup of cannabis-infused coconut oil, ¼ cup of organic olive oil, ⅓ cup of beeswax/cocoa butter/shea butter. Once this is completely melted, add a few drops of essential oil and mix well. Pour the mixture into a bowl and let it cool to room temperature. With a hand mixer, whip the salve until completely smooth and then transfer into salve containers. You can find these at a craft supply store. I suggest choosing pretty containers and/or decorating them so that they are gift ready.

Cannabis Lube

Cannabis lube (or "pre-lube," to be exact) is a new product that is targeted at women to make orgasms more intense and more frequent. This product is a cannabis oil spray that you spray onto your clitoris 15–30 minutes before sex. Wait until you feel that the medicine has "activated" your clit and then . . . go! By topically applying the cannabis oil, one company claims, you are increasing blood flow and nerve sensation, which can enhance your sensual experience. I suggest using your cannabis-infused coconut oil as a DIY pre-lube. If you want to make it fancy, infuse it with a small amount of lavender essential oil and store it in a pretty jar. Also, this pre-lube is not condom compatible.

Cannabis Tincture

Making cannabis tincture is extremely easy and deeply satisfying at the same time. Cannabis tincture makes a great gift, and it is a quick and easy way to get high. You will need alcohol (grain alcohol, vodka, or red wine all work just fine), a quart size glass jar, a glass bowl, cheese cloth, a rubber band, a tiny funnel, 6–8 2 oz dark colored tincture bottles, plastic gloves, stickers for labeling your bottles, parchment paper, and a baking sheet. The first step is decarboxylating your trim. Start by turning your oven on to 240 degrees. Next, you will need to grab some trim from the cool, dark place where it is being stored. Depending on how strong you want your tincture, you can use as little as ½ cup or as much as you can pack into your quart jar. Next, line your baking sheet with parchment paper and sprinkle your trim evenly across the paper. Put the trim into the oven for 20–30 minutes. This process of decarboxylating your trim will activate the resin and convert the molecules of THC into a form that makes it psychoactive when you ingest it. Let the trim cool and then pour it into your jar. Pour your alcohol over the trim so that it completely fills the jar with trim and liquid. Next, screw on the cap and set the jar in a cool, dark place where it will live for 30–60 days. Shake the jar once a week. Once the alcohol is thoroughly infused with cannabis, unscrew the lid and secure 2 layers of cheese cloth over the mouth of the jar, using the rubber band. Pour the liquid into the glass bowl and discard the trim. Pour the liquid, with the help of the tiny funnel, into the tincture bottles. Screw the tincture bottles closed and label each bottle. Store in a cool, dark place out of the reach of children. To use your tincture, start by taking a few drops and waiting a few minutes and increase your dosage over time, as desired. While grain alcohol will make a stronger tincture, a tincture made from wine will be far more palatable.

Part Five

HASH
MAKING

When I told a friend of mine about my interest in the intersection of feminism and cannabis, she shared a beautiful story with me. She had been in a relationship with a man for several years who was controlling and verbally abusive. He did not approve of her smoking weed, so she abstained from cannabis and all psychedelic substances during the course of their relationship. They ended up taking a trip together to Egypt, and it occurred to her that there were people all around her smoking hash. She loves weed and decided that she was going to take advantage of this opportunity. She remembers smoking hash and coming to a full-bodied awareness that she was in an oppressive relationship and that she needed to leave. She broke up with her boyfriend and now works as a consultant in the cannabis industry. There is no guarantee that smoking hash will catalyze you to break chains of oppression and realize your dreams, but for this friend, this was her experience.

Hash is the concentration of resin glands, which contain the psychoactive THC that makes you stoned. You can make hash by rubbing flowers between your fingers, by agitating plant material in cold water, or by extracting the resin from plant material with the use of butane or CO_2. Regardless of which method you use, the aim is to remove the resin glands from the flowers in order to have a concentrated form of THC, which is called hash. As far as I am concerned, there are three reasons to make hash: 1) you can make use of all your trim and b-buds instead of composting them, 2) it is easier to make canna-butter or coconut oil for edibles with hash than it is with raw plant material, and 3) you might really like smoking hash or have friends who do.

I will describe how to make hash using a cold water extraction method. This process will result in what is known as "bubble hash" because it bubbles when it is smoked. Bubble hash is known as solventless cannabis extract because it is free of neurotoxic chemical solvents, such as butane or hexane, which are commonly used to make hash oil. Beware—most cannabis vape pen cartridges use hash oil that was extracted with butane. Unbelievable. If vaping with hash oil is your thing and you are interested in a safer alternative, I recommend buying cartridges that either use Rosin (which is solventless!) or CO_2 extracted oil.

Cold water extraction is the process of using cold water to make resin glands brittle and then agitating plant material so that the glands break off and separate from the plant material. Next you will use "bubble bags," which are nylon bags with screens that have holes of varying diameters, to catch and separate plant matter and resin glands. The micron size refers to the size of the holes in each screen. The smaller the micron size, the smaller the holes in the screen.

After trimming, you will have lots of trim, which are the little particles of leaf that have been snipped off of the buds. Sifting through trim is always heart-wrenching for me because I can see all of the glittering trichomes rich with THC and CBD, and I hate to throw away all of that psychoactive and healing material. One way of using that trim is by turning it into cold water hash. You can do this at any time over the course of the following year; however, hash connoisseurs swear that hash made with fresh trim tastes better. I will describe two basic methods of making cold water hash.

In this section I will describe how to make hash, first using simple, cheap tools, and then I will describe how to make hash using a fairly expensive machine. If you are experimenting with making hash for your first time, you do not intend to make enormous amounts of it regularly, and/or you want to make your hash as cheaply as possible, I recommend following the instructions for the first method. However, if you know that you love hash, you want to make it easily, and money is not an issue, then I recommend buying a machine and following the second set of instructions. I bought a machine because I was making lots of hash that I was going to use in my artisanal cannabis-infused chocolates that I was going to sell to dispensaries. Unfortunately, the permitting process became far too burdensome for a small chocolatier like myself to wade through, and so the project came to an end. However, now I have enough experience with both hash making methods to teach you!

THE MANUAL METHOD

The manual method of hash making uses cheap and easy to find tools. However, this method is more labor intensive than the second method that I describe, where you rely on a machine to do most of the work for you. For both the manual and machine methods, you will need to work in a place that can get wet, such as a garage, on a deck, or somewhere in your backyard. You will also need a place to dump lots of trim, such as a compost pile, and a place to dump lots of hash-infused water.

You start the manual method with pouring your dry plant material, which is free of all sticks, into the clean trash can. Pour in a few bags of ice—the larger the ice cubes the better. Pour in water until it covers the ice and leaf material. Use the coldest water you possibly can.

Next, you are going to agitate the mix with a paint mixer attached to a drill. You can purchase paint mixers at most hardware stores; make sure to find one that is durable with a very long stem. You are going to agitate the ice water and plant material for 15 minutes. One trick for doing this is using a zip tie to keep the trigger pulled: just wrap it around the handle and over the trigger and cinch it tight. This will prevent your trigger finger from becoming fatigued.

Material Lists

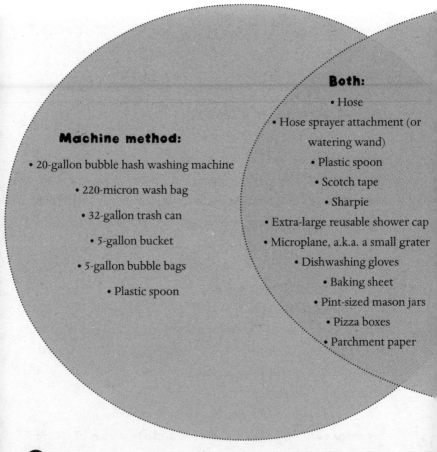

Machine method:

• 20-gallon bubble hash washing machine

• 220-micron wash bag

• 32-gallon trash can

• 5-gallon bucket

• 5-gallon bubble bags

• Plastic spoon

Both:

• Hose

• Hose sprayer attachment (or watering wand)

• Plastic spoon

• Scotch tape

• Sharpie

• Extra-large reusable shower cap

• Microplane, a.k.a. a small grater

• Dishwashing gloves

• Baking sheet

• Pint-sized mason jars

• Pizza boxes

• Parchment paper

The ice will begin to melt. You want the water to remain extremely cold, so if there is less than ¼ of the original amount of ice you put into the bucket or trash can left after mixing for a while, replenish the ice and return it to at least ½ of the original amount.

Keeping the water extremely cold allows the trichomes to remain brittle and easily broken off when agitated. Agitate again for 15 more minutes.

Manual method:

- 2 clean 32-gallon trash cans on wheels
- 2-gallon bucket
- Paint mixer with long stem that can be used as a drill attachment
- Drill
- 20-gallon bubble bags[1]
- Wheelbarrow (optional)
- Ice tray or a silicone mini-cupcake tray
- Baking sheet

---

1 Bubble bags are nylon bags lined with mesh screens on the bottom of each. The mesh has screen sizes that vary from large to tiny, and these screens catch different sized trichomes. These bags are typically bought in sets of 3, 5, or 7 and in 5- or 20-gallon sizes.

The next step is to take your bubble bags and fit them inside of a second clean plastic trash can, making sure that you fold the top of each bag over the lip of the can. You will want each bag to fit onto the trash can securely. If your bags have drawstrings, pull them tightly so that the bags hold tightly onto the top of the trash can. You are going to stack your bags into the can or bucket, starting with the bags with the smallest size microns, which are the bags with the smallest number. If you have a 7-bag set, put your 25-micron bag on first, your 45 on next, and so on. Your top bag will be your 220 bag. If you think about this for a second, it makes sense. Large particles and plant debris get caught in the top few bags and smaller particles make their way down to the bags that were stacked first. These bags with the smallest microns, the 25-micron bags, will collect the smallest sized trichomes, which are prized within the cold water hash community.

This next part can get messy, so make sure that you are working in a place where you and the floor can get wet. You will need a 2-gallon bucket. Use the bucket to scoop the trim/ice water out of the trash can and pour it into the bags that are hanging in the second trash can. Scoop out as much of the plant/ice/water mix as you can and for the last bit; you will need to pick up the trash can and dump the remaining contents into the bubble bags hanging in the second trash can. This is potentially really heavy, so you might need a friend to help you, unless you are some sort of CrossFit queen.

Keep your friend around for this next part. You will need to lift up the top bubble bag, which will be your 220-micron bag, and remove it from the trash can. It will be full of trim, ice, and some water. You will need to shake it up and down to release all of the water from it. Quick, hard thrusts work the best for getting the water out of the bag. Dump all of the ice and trim into the compost. I like to have a wheelbarrow around that I can dump my trim into and then wheel it to my compost pile. There will be low quality hash in this bag, but it will be mixed with lots of plant material. This hash will taste foul and will easily mold, so just discard it. Once your bag is empty, use your watering wand to spray your bag clean. Hang your bag to dry in a clean place.

You will lift the next bag in the same way that you lifted your 220 bag. Lift it out of the water and then jerk it up and down until all of the water has drained out. I will emphasize that you really want to get as much moisture out as possible. Then, hang the bag from the first trash can that you used by folding the top of the bag over the lip of the trash can. It should hang like a trash bag.

Take your hose with a spray attachment or watering wand and gently spray the remaining material away from the edges of the bag and into a clump in the middle of the bottom of the bag. This material is hash! Be patient and spray very gently. Let the clump sit for a minute so that any remaining moisture can drain out. Next, use a plastic spoon to scoop the hash out of the bag and into an ice tray or a silicone mini-cupcake tray. These silicon cupcake cups are amazing because the hash does not stick to them and it creates these perfect little cakes that are easy to work with in the next stage. I suggest using a plastic spoon because after using it to scoop hash you will want to throw it away. Make sure to label each cup with the strain and micron number of the bag that it was collected from. I recommend writing the info on Scotch tape with a Sharpie and sticking that next to the cup that you are labeling.

Finally, use the hose to clean out the bag once you have scooped it clean of hash. Hang your bag out to dry.

You will repeat this process for each of the remaining bags: lift out of the water, shake out all of the moisture, hang the bag in the first trash can, spray the hash to the middle of the screen, scoop out the hash, rinse out the bag, and hang it to dry. Repeat. The final two bags are usually very difficult to lift because the microns are very small and the water has a difficult time draining out of these bags. You will end up lifting lots of water, and the jerking motion will not release as much water as it did with previous bags. I wish I had a tip to make this part easier. Oh wait, I do! But that comes later.

Once all of your hash has been scooped into cupcake cups and labeled, place an extra-large shower cap over the silicon tray, set this on a baking sheet to give the silicon tray stability, and set this in the freezer. Leave the hash in the freezer until each cup is completely frozen. Once frozen, you can store the cakes in small mason jars, but remember to transfer the labels. You can leave these in the freezer until you are ready for the second stage of processing. Finally, wheel your trash can full of water to your water-dumping location. Ideally, you can use this water for something, like watering a tree or your winter garden. Rinse all of the buckets, trash cans, spoons, etc.

Heavy Bag Solution

Materials:

- 5-gallon bucket with the bottom cut off
- 32-gallon trash can on wheels, with a flat lid
- 5-gallon bubble bags

There is a trick for dealing with heavy bags. This requires a slightly different setup for stacking and pulling bags. You will need a flat lid which fits securely onto your clean, 32-gallon trash can. With a jig saw, you will cut a hole in the top of the lid, where you will place a 5-gallon bucket. You will also need to cut the bottom off of the 5-gallon bucket. For this method, you will use 5-gallon bags and fit them into the 5-gallon bucket, which is sitting snugly in the hole of the flat trash can lid, which fits securely onto the 32-gallon trash can. You will either scoop or drain your trim ice water into the 5-gallon bags, depending on whether you are using the manual or machine method. The water will drain through the bags and into the trash can. If you scoop it, you will probably need to empty your top bag into the compost several times during the process. Make sure when you re-hang it that the outside of the bag is completely clean. You do not want to get trim into the bag hanging below the 220-micron bag. At this point, all of the water has drained through the 5-gallon bags and into the 32-gallon trash can below.

Next, just go through the steps listed above for collecting hash from each bag. Because the bags are smaller, it will be a million times easier to work with them. I did not invent this; I discovered it on the internet.

MACHINE METHOD

The second method of doing this agitation process is by buying a cold water hash washing machine. These are known as bubble machines. They are truly wonderful little machines. They can cost $150 or more, depending on the size you want to use. The instructions here are for a 20-gallon machine. You will need a 220-micron wash bag, which, if it does not come with the machine or your bubble bag set, you will need to order. The 220 wash bag is different than the bubble bags in that you put all of your trim inside of it, zip it closed, and then you can throw it into your cold water hash washing machine. These are very easy to find on the internet.

When you set up your hash washing machine, make sure that the plug can reach an outlet and that the machine is in reach of a hose. Next, pour ice into the bottom of the washtub, enough ice to cover the bottom of the machine. Fill your wash bag with trim and put the full bag into the machine. Fill the rest of the machine with ice and cover the ice and bag with water. Set the timer on the machine and walk away.

I have run the machine for long periods (30 minutes) and have repeated the "wash cycle" several times in a row, each time adding more ice, in order to extract as much hash as possible. I highly recommend this method if maximizing yields is important to you. Also, when deciding whether to buy a machine or use the paint mixer method, do take into consideration that your yields will be enormously better—at least twice as good—if you use the machine.

If you choose to buy the bubble machine, you will follow the same directions with hanging your bubble bags in a clean trash can, but instead of scooping the trim/ice/water into the bags with a small bucket, the bubble machine has a pump that will pump that water into the bags for you. You simply put the drain tube into your 220 bag and the machine will pump all of the cold water into your bag. Your trim will remain in the 220-micron wash bag. You can pull that out and compost the trim. Make sure to rinse off your wash bag and hang it to dry.

Next, you will follow the directions listed above for extracting hash. All of the other steps will remain the same.

Second Stage of Hash Processing

Once the bags are clean, the trim composted, the water poured out somewhere, and the hash labeled and frozen, it is time to set up the second step.

You will need clean pizza boxes, parchment paper, a "microplane" (a.k.a. a small grater), and dishwashing gloves. Line a pizza box with parchment paper. Put on the dishwashing gloves and pull a single frozen hash cake from the freezer. Put the label that was next to the cake onto the pizza box so that it is now labeled with the strain and micron size of the hash that it will contain. Next, grate the cake onto the parchment paper.

Work quickly and in the coldest conditions possible, because you really want the cake to remain frozen as you grate it. I recommend freezing the grater in preparation for this process to help keep the cake frozen.

As you grate onto the parchment paper, move the grater around to ensure that you spread the shavings equally across the paper. You do not want to end up with a pile of shavings, as this will affect how the hash dries. Be very careful while you grate the last bit of frozen hash cake. You do not want to grate your gloves and end up with plastic in your hash. Once your hash cake is completely grated, close the top of the pizza box and set it in a dry, clean place, like your dry room, an attic, or a closet. The hash should be dry in 7 days, more or less. Do not rush this process and do not attempt to remove it from the parchment until it is bone dry.

Once the hash is completely dry, it is ready to cure. For this process, you will need a small mason jar. Collect all of the hash from your pizza box and transfer this into a jar. Move the label from the pizza box to the jar and seal the lid closed. Repeat this process for each pizza box. Store your jars in a cool, dark place. Burp your jars every few weeks over the course of a few months. At this point, you can smoke the hash, use it to make canna-coconut oil, or make rosin with it. Rosin is a type of dab, or cannabis oil, made from cold water hash.

If you have kept each micron batch separate, then the batches pulled from the smallest micron size will be a lighter color, or "blonde," and theoretically they will taste better. Is this just racism? Probably, but also, hash pulled from bags with small micron sizes will have a higher concentration of resin than hash pulled from bags with larger microns. This means that the hash is purer and should taste better.

It is very important to note that what goes into your hash is what comes out. If you put old, moldy trim that smells bad through this process, you will end up with moldy, bad-smelling hash. If you start with fresh, single strain trim full of b-buds and you follow the directions closely, you will end up with an amazing product that you will be very proud of.

Some "extract artists" are committed to using only fresh material. This means using fresh cannabis flowers, freezing them, and then running the frozen material through the process instead of dried trim. I have tried this method, but my yields were so low that I was discouraged and never tried it again. Also, I do not have a palate that is nearly sensitive enough to discern between a hash made with dry trim and hash made from fresh frozen material. I have a pedestrian palate, and I am OK with that. However, if this sparks your interest and you end up with a product that you love, more power to you!

Conclusion

"Celebrate this ordinary event
of disintegration
disorientation
this moment before the beginning."
- Madrone Stewart

The end of your first season of cultivation is a time to slow down. Temperatures have dropped and rain is falling. You might even be blessed with snowfall. Now is the time to pull out your cozy blankets, turn the kettle on, and start bingeing on Netflix (or, for god's sake, make some art!). For cannabis cultivators, winter is a quiet time in which we can reflect on the past cultivation season and prepare for the upcoming year. This winter will mark the end of your first season growing outdoors and the beginning of a lifetime of cultivating cannabis and, hopefully, many other nourishing and psychoactive plants.

Winter is the perfect time to pull out your laptop and record notes from this past year. What worked really well and what seriously failed? Were there strains you were happier with than others? Ultimately, what would you like to do different next year and what do you want to keep the same? All of your "mistakes" from this year can become lessons for your upcoming year if you can come up with solutions for those problems now. Assessing this past year will inevitably overlap with planning for your upcoming year. I encourage you to make a second document where you can start jotting down plans.

Along with assessing and planning, now is the time to buy seeds. If you get really excited, you can start collecting irrigation parts and supplies you will need for spring. However, no matter how excited you get about your next season, I strongly advise against starting your seeds before March. Starting before March will require lights and will put your seeds at risk for developing fungal problems.

I have one last suggestion for wrapping up last year. I want to encourage you to give your flowers away. You should certainly hold on to as much of your harvest as you need for your personal use.

However, if you have any sense of a surplus, I strongly encourage you to gift flowers, hash, tinctures, lube, edibles, and salve to friends and family. There are few greater gifts that you can give than the plant medicine that you grew with love, under the sun. This is a rare opportunity for you to contribute to the physical and psychological wellness of your community. You have the opportunity to be a community herbalist, and this is a special privilege. I guarantee that giving flowers away will enhance your relationship with your garden, as it transforms you from simply a cannabis consumer to a medicine provider. You get to be that herbalist/witch/shaman/root doctor you always wanted to be!

Winter is also a fantastic time to dive deep inside of your mind with the help of the cannabis that you grew. I strongly suggest altering your mind with the intention of cultivating insight, joy, and relaxation. I also suggest altering your mind in a place where you feel comfortable and safe. The best way to induce paranoia and/or a bad trip is by getting high in a sketchy place. With the right mindset and setting, you can tap into the phenomenal power that this plant medicine has to offer to your personal growth and your perspective on social and cultural constructs. This world needs as many "woke" women as it can get, and if cannabis helps you to shift your mind so that you can wake up to your own power, your dreams, internalized oppressions, and strategies for liberation, then I want you to take time out to get high. If cannabis helps you to feel more creative, more in tune with yourself and your community, and/or if it helps you relax in the midst of this world full of suffering, then I hope that you take time out to connect with this mystical plant medicine. If cannabis empowers, relaxes, brings joy and insight to you, then I wholeheartedly encourage you to set aside time to enjoy smoking weed as a feminist experience.

This book is a gift to you, and I hope that you have learned something from the words tucked between its covers. This book was not written for your academic exploration of cannabis cultivation. It is intended to motivate you to actually do things in this world. It is a call to action! I would like nothing more than for you to get into your garden and experiment with what you have learned here. I hope that you experiment with germinating seeds, paying close attention to the life cycle of your plants, smoking your own homegrown weed, and extending the spirit of generosity to your community. I hope that you use your cannabis to take psychonautic adventures that are empowering and liberating. I hope that these experiments are successful and that you emerge from this experience feeling happier, healthier, and stronger. I also hope that all of us home growers give dispensaries a run for their money. Why let them control the medicine supply when we can happily cultivate our own? Have fun out there!

TWENTY IDEAS FOR ENRICHING YOUR CANNABIS GROWING EXPERIENCE

1. Listen to music while you are gardening.
2. If you are a musician, sing or play your instrument in your garden.
3. Name your plants.
4. Decorate your garden with strings of lights, art, and prayer flags.
5. Set up an altar in your garden.
6. Meditate and chant in your garden.
7. Work mindfully, in silence.
8. Photograph your plants.
9. Draw or paint illustrations of your plants.
10. Plant other plants in your garden, especially those that you can eat, those that heal, those that are beautiful, and those that smell delicious.
11. Journal as you move through the seasons.
12. Make art inspired by your cultivation experience.
13. Read in your garden.
14. Smoke weed in your garden.
15. Do yoga in your garden.
16. Make love in your garden.
17. On hot days in late summer, when your plants are big, sit underneath them in the shade.
18. Relax and have fun. Do not let this project stress you out.
19. Schedule time to spend in your garden, slowly checking on plant health, looking for pests, and connecting with your plants.
20. Invite close friends and loved ones to help you in your garden (but have them swear to secrecy)

ABOUT THE AUTHOR

Madrone Stewart is a writer, community counselor, feminist weed farmer and owner of Purple Kite Farm. She lives on her sailboat in Oakland, CA.